# DANIEL

*God's Control over Rulers and Nations*

JOHN
MacARTHUR

Daniel
MacArthur Bible Studies

© 2000, John F. MacArthur, Jr. All rights reserved. No portion of this book may be reproduced, stored in a retrieval system, or transmitted in any form or by any means—electronic, mechanical, photocopy, recording, or any other— except for brief quotations in printed reviews, without the prior permission of the publisher.

John MacArthur
"Unleashing God's Truth, One Verse at a Time®"
"Unleashing God's Truth, One Verse at a Time" is a trademark of Grace to You. All rights reserved.

Published in Nashville, Tennessee, by Thomas Nelson. Thomas Nelson is a registered trademark of Thomas Nelson, Inc.

Scripture passages taken from:
The Holy Bible, *New King James Version*
© 1979, 1980, 1982 by Thomas Nelson. All rights reserved.

Cover Art by The Puckett Group.
Interior design and composition by Design Corps, Batavia, IL.

Produced with the assistance of the Livingstone Corporation. Project staff include Dave Veerman, Christopher D. Hudson, and Amber Rae.

Project editor: Len Woods

ISBN 978-0-8499-5542-6

All rights reserved. *Printed in the United States of America.*

HB 12.21.2017

# The Book of Daniel

## Table of Contents

# THE BOOK OF DANIEL

## Introduction

According to Hebrew custom, the title is drawn from the prophet who throughout the book received revelations from God. Daniel bridges the entire seventy years of the Babylonian captivity (605–536 B.C.; see 1:1 and 9:1–3). Nine of the twelve chapters relate revelation through dreams and visions. Daniel was God's mouthpiece to the Gentile and Jewish world, declaring God's current and future plans. What Revelation is to the New Testament prophetically and apocalyptically, Daniel is to the Old Testament.

## Author and Date

Several verses indicate that Daniel, whose name means "God is my Judge," wrote this book (8:15, 27; 9:2; 10:2,7;12:4–5). He wrote in the autobiographical first person from 7:2 on and should be distinguished from the other three Daniels of the Old Testament (see 1 Chronicles 3:1; Ezra 8:2; Nehemiah 10:6). As a teenager, possibly about fifteen years old, Daniel was taken captive, virtually kidnapped, from his noble family in Judah. He and other young Jewish men were deported to Babylon to be brainwashed into Babylonian culture for the task of assisting in dealing with the imported Jews. There Daniel spent the rest of his life (eighty-five years or more) and made the most of the exile, successfully exalting God by his character and service. Daniel quickly rose to the role of statesman by official royal appointment and served as a confidante of kings as well as a prophet in two world empires—the Babylonian (2:48) and the Medo-Persian (6:1–2). Also, Christ confirmed Daniel as the author of this book (Matthew 24:15).

Daniel lived beyond the time described in 10:1 (536 B.C.) It seems most probable that he wrote the book shortly after this date but before 530 B.C.. The passage in 2:4b to 7:28, which prophetically describes the course of Gentile world history, was originally and appropriately written in Aramaic, the contemporary language of international business. Ezekiel, Habakkuk, Jeremiah, and Zephaniah were Daniel's contemporaries.

## Background and Setting

The book begins in 605 B.C. when Babylon conquered Jerusalem and exiled Daniel, his three friends, and many others. It continues to the eventual demise of Babylonian supremacy in 539 B.C., when Medo-Persian besiegers conquered Babylon (5:30–31), and goes even beyond that to 536 B.C. (10:1).

After Daniel was transported to Babylon, the Babylonian victors conquered Jerusalem in two further stages (597 BC and 586 BC). In both takeovers, they deported more Jewish captives. Daniel passionately remembered his home, particularly the temple at Jerusalem, almost seventy years after having been taken away from it (6:10).

Jeremiah alludes to Daniel's background as it names three of the last five kings in Judah before captivity (see Jeremiah 1:1–3): Josiah (641–609 B.C.), Jehoiakim (609–598 B.C.) and Zedekiah (597–586 B.C.). Jehoahaz (609 B.C.) and Jehoiachin (598–597 B.C.) are not mentioned. Daniel is also mentioned by Ezekiel (see 14:14, 20; 28:3) as being righteous and wise. The book of Hebrews also alludes to Daniel as one of "the prophets: who through faith . . . stopped the mouths of lions" (Hebrews 11:32-33).

The long-continued sin of the Judeans without national repentance eventually led to God's judgment of which Jeremiah, Habakkuk, and Zephaniah had given fair warning. Earlier, Isaiah and other faithful prophets of God had also trumpeted the danger. When Assyrian power had ebbed by 625 B.C., the Neo-Babylonians conquered: (1) Assyria with its capital Nineveh in 612 B.C.; (2) Egypt in the following years; (3) Judah in 605 B.C. when they overthrew Jerusalem in the first of three steps (also in 597 B.C. and 586 B.C.). Daniel was in one of the first groups of deportees; Ezekiel followed in 597 B.C.

Israel, the northern kingdom, had earlier fallen to Assyria in 722 B.C. With Judah's captivity, the judgment was complete. In Babylon, Daniel received God's word concerning successive stages of Gentile world domination through the centuries until the greatest Conqueror, Messiah, would reign. He would defeat all foes and raise His covenant people to blessing in His glorious millennial kingdom.

# Historical and Theological Themes

Daniel was written to encourage the exiled Jews by revealing God's program for them, both during and after the time of Gentile power in the world. Prominent above every other theme in the book is God's sovereign control over the affairs of all rulers and nations, and their final replacement with the True King. The key verses are 2:20–22, 44 (see also, 2:28, 37; 4:34–35; 6:25–27). God had not suffered defeat in allowing Israel's fall (chapter 1) but was providentially working His sure purposes toward a full display of His King, the exalted Christ. God sovereignly allowed Gentiles to dominate Israel—that is, Babylon (605–539 B.C.), Medo-Persia (539–331 B.C.), Greece (331–146 B.C.), Rome (146 B.C.–A.D. 476), and all the way to the Second Advent of Christ. These stages in Gentile power are set forth in chapters 2 and 7. This same theme also embraces Israel's experience both in defeat and finally in her kingdom blessing in chapters 8–12 (see 2:35, 45; 7:27). A key aspect within the over-arching theme of God's kingly control is Messiah's coming to rule the world in glory over all men (see 2:35, 45; 7:13, 14, 27). He is like a stone in chapter 2 and like a son of man in chapter 7. In addition, He is the Anointed One (Messiah) in chapter 9:26. Chapter 9 provides the chronological framework from Daniel's time to Christ's kingdom.

A second theme woven into the fabric of Daniel is the display of God's sovereign power through miracles. Daniel's era is one of six in the Bible with a major focus on miracles by which God accomplished His purposes. Other periods include: (1) the Creation and Flood (Genesis 1–11); (2) the patriarchs and Moses (Genesis 12—Deuteronomy); (3) Elijah and Elisha (1 Kings 19—2 Kings 13); (4) Jesus and the apostles (Gospels, Acts); (5) the time of the Second Advent (Revelation).

God, who has everlasting dominion and ability to work according to His will (4:34–35), is capable of miracles, all of which would be lesser displays of power than was exhibited when He acted as Creator in Genesis 1:1. Daniel chronicles the God-enabled recounting and interpreting of dreams that God used to reveal His will (chapters 2, 4, 7). Other miracles include: (1) his protection of the three men in the blazing furnace (chapter 3); (2) His writing on the wall and Daniel's interpreting it (chapter 5); (3) His provision of safety for

Daniel in a lions' den (chapter 6); and (4) supernatural prophecies (chapter 2; chapter 7; chapter 8; 9:24–12:13).

## Interpretive Challenges

The main challenges center on interpreting passages about future tribulation and kingdom promises. Though the use of Imperial Aramaic and archeology have confirmed the early date of writing, some skeptical interpreters, unwilling to acknowledge the possibility of any supernatural prophecies, place these details in the intertestamental times. They see these prophecies not as miraculously foretelling the future but as simply the observations of a later writer, who is recording events of his own day. Thus, these skeptics date Daniel in the days of Antiochus IV Epiphanes (175–164 B.C.—see chapter 8; 11:21–45). According to this scheme, the expectation of the Stone and Son of Man (chapters 2 and 7) turned out to be a mistaken notion that did not actually come to pass, or the writer was being intentionally deceptive.

Actually, a future seven-year judgment period (see 7:21–22; 11:36–45; 12:1) and a literal thousand-year kingdom (see Revelation 20) after Christ's second coming when He will reign over Israelites and Gentiles (7:27) are taught. This will be an era before and distinct from the final, absolutely perfect, ultimate state that is, the new heaven and the new earth with its capital, the New Jerusalem (Revelation 21–22). The literal interpretation of prophecy, including Daniel, leads to the premillennial perspective.

Many other aspects of interpretation challenge readers: for example, interpreting the numbers used (1:12, 20; 3:19; 9:24–27); identifying the "One like a Son of Man" (7:13–14); determining whether to see Antiochus of the past or Antichrist of the far future in 8:19–23; explaining the "seventy sevens" in 9:24–27; deciding whether Antiochus of 11:21–35 is still meant in 11:36–45, or whether it refers to the future Antichrist.

# Daniel and His Friends Obey God

Daniel 1:1–21

## Opening Thought

1) It's true that hard times and crises not only build character, they also reveal it. In other words, how a person handles difficulties says a lot about that person's character and beliefs.

What's the most difficult situation you've ever had to face? How did you handle it? What did it reveal about your faith?

_____

_____

_____

_____

_____

_____

2) What tests or trials are you facing right now? Are you clinging to God and continuing to faithfully live as He commands? Or are you compromising? Grade yourself (A–F) and explain why you gave yourself that grade.

_____

_____

_____

_____

_____

_____

# Background of the Passage

By piecing together evidence from the biblical record we can conclude that Daniel likely grew up in a godly home, his parents having been impacted by the spiritual revival and cultural reforms spearheaded by King Josiah. Surely it was disheartening for this prominent Jewish family to watch as Judah's brief repentance was snuffed out by the wicked kings Jehoahaz and then Jehoiakim.

Despite faithful prophets like Jeremiah, the nation staggered toward certain judgment. Chapter 1 describes this regrettable turn of events— Nebuchadnezzar's conquest of Jerusalem (1:1–2) and his conscription of the most gifted and talented Jews to serve in the royal court in Babylon (1:3–7).

The balance of the chapter (and really the entire book) tells of four young Hebrew teenagers under duress (1:8–16). Daniel, Hananiah, Mishael, and Azariah were in a strange land far from home. They had been ripped away from their families, friends, beloved religious customs, from all that they had ever known. Suddenly they were among pagans in a land teeming with idols and decadence.

How would they fare? How would they deal with emotions like fear and sorrow and anger? Would they keep the faith? Would they compromise? Would they become bitter? Would they cave in to despair . . . or rise to the occasion?

This is a wonder chapter, an encouraging look at some rare young men of integrity. Here are great lessons about purity and principle. Here we can learn much about standing tall and strong in the midst of great trial.

The chapter closes with these four young heroes having passed the test. God has honored their faithfulness. They are chosen for royal positions (1:17–21). This will give them a platform for future effectiveness and an international impact.

# Bible Passage

Read 1:1–21, noting the key words and definitions to the right of the passage.

## Daniel 1:1–21

**1** In the third year of the reign of Jehoiakim king of Judah, Nebuchadnezzar king of Babylon came to Jerusalem and besieged it.

**2** And the Lord gave Jehoiakim king of Judah into his hand, with some of the articles of the house of God, which he carried into the land of Shinar to the house of his god; and he brought the articles into the treasure house of his god.

**3** Then the king instructed Ashpenaz, the master of his eunuchs, to bring some of the children of Israel and some of the king's descendants and some of the nobles,

**4** young men in whom there was no blemish, but good-looking, gifted in all wisdom, possessing knowledge and quick to understand, who had ability to serve in the king's palace, and whom they might teach the language and literature of the Chaldeans.

**5** And the king appointed for them a daily provision of the king's delicacies and of the wine which he drank, and three years of training for them, so that at the end of that time they might serve before the king.

**6** Now from among those of the sons of Judah were Daniel, Hananiah, Mishael, and Azariah.

**7** To them the chief of the eunuchs gave names: he gave Daniel the name Belteshazzar; to Hananiah, Shadrach; to Mishael, Meshach; and to Azariah, Abed-Nego.

**8** But Daniel purposed in his heart that he would not defile himself with the portion of the king's delicacies, nor with the wine which he drank; therefore he requested of the chief of the eunuchs that he might not defile himself.

**9** Now God had brought Daniel into the favor and goodwill of the chief of the eunuchs.

**10** And the chief of the eunuchs said to Daniel, "I fear my lord the king, who has appointed your food and drink. For why should he see your faces

**third year** (v. 1)—606–605 B.C., the third year by Babylonian dating, which did not count a king's initial (accession) year, but began with the following year; so the "third year" is in harmony with the same year labeled as "fourth" by the Judean system of dating

**Jehoiakim** (v. 1)—the wicked son of Josiah who ruled Judah (609–597 B.C.) during Nebuchadnezzar's first plundering of Jerusalem

**Nebuchadnezzar** (v. 1)—the son of Nabopolassar, who ruled Babylon from 605–562 b.c.

**Shinar** (v. 2)—a term for Babylon

**his god** (v. 2)—Bel or Marduk; the Babylonians were polytheistic and believed their military victories demonstrated the superiority of their deities over those of their enemies

**young men** (v. 4)—probably between the ages of fourteen and seventeen

**gave names** (v. 7)—a key factor in the Babylonian attempt to "brainwash" their captives; they tried to completely separate them from their pasts

**Daniel . . . Belteshazzar** (v. 7) —Daniel means "God is my Judge." Belteshazzar means "Bel Protect the King."

**Hananiah . . . Shadrach** (v. 7) —Hananiah means "the Lord is Gracious." Shadrach means "Command of Aku" (another Babylonian god).

**Mishael . . . Meshach** (v. 7) —Mishael means "Who is like the Lord?" Meshach means "Who is what Aku is?"

**Azariah . . . Abednego** (v. 7) —Azariah means "the Lord is my

looking worse than the young men who are your age? Then you would endanger my head before the king."

**11** So Daniel said to the steward whom the chief of the eunuchs had set over Daniel, Hananiah, Mishael, and Azariah,

**12** "Please test your servants for ten days, and let them give us vegetables to eat and water to drink.

**13** "Then let our appearance be examined before you, and the appearance of the young men who eat the portion of the king's delicacies; and as you see fit, so deal with your servants."

**14** So he consented with them in this matter, and tested them ten days.

**15** And at the end of ten days their features appeared better and fatter in flesh than all the young men who ate the portion of the king's delicacies.

**16** Thus the steward took away their portion of delicacies and the wine that they were to drink, and gave them vegetables.

**17** As for these four young men, God gave them knowledge and skill in all literature and wisdom; and Daniel had understanding in all visions and dreams.

**18** Now at the end of the days, when the king had said that they should be brought in, the chief of the eunuchs brought them in before Nebuchadnezzar.

**19** Then the king interviewed them, and among them all none was found like Daniel, Hananiah, Mishael, and Azariah; therefore they served before the king.

**20** And in all matters of wisdom and understanding about which the king examined them, he found them ten times better than all the magicians and astrologers who were in all his realm.

**21** Thus Daniel continued until the first year of King Cyrus.

Helper." Abednego means "Servant of Nego" (or Nebo, the god of vegetation).

**Daniel purposed** (v. 8)—Daniel (together with three fellow Hebrew captives) resolved not to violate Jewish law by eating the pagan foods that had been devoted to idols. For them to have indulged would have been to honor these false gods.

**Now God had brought Daniel into . . . favor** (v. 9)—God honored Daniel's trust and allegiance by sovereignly working favorably for him among the heathen leaders; he was able to earn their respect.

**vegetables** (v. 12)—This Hebrew word may refer strictly to fresh vegetables; it might also include wheat or barley.

**fatter in flesh** (v. 15)—an indicator of healthiness

**ten times better** (v. 20)—This number is probably used qualitatively to signify fullness or completeness. The idea is that the young Hebrew men displayed incredible skill and surpassed the other trainees because of the favor of their God.

**first year** (v. 21)—Cyrus of Persia conquered Babylon in 539 B.C.; his third year (mentioned in 10:1), is the latest historical year mentioned by Daniel (see Ezra 1:1—2:1).

# Understanding the Text

3) What happened to Judah when it was besieged by the Babylonians? Why did God allow this?

_____

_____

_____

_____

_____

(verses to consider: Jeremiah 26–27)

4) For what qualities did the Babylonians look when selecting candidates from among the Hebrews for potential royal service?

_____

_____

_____

_____

5) Why did Daniel ask his Babylonian captors for a vegetarian diet? What happened as a result? Why do you think this incident was included in inspired Scripture?

_____

_____

_____

_____

_____

# Cross Reference

Read about the historical background of chapter 1 in 2 Kings 23:34—24:6:

³⁴ *Then Pharaoh Necho made Eliakim the son of Josiah king in place of his father Josiah, and changed his name to Jehoiakim. And Pharaoh took Jehoahaz and went to Egypt, and he died there.*

³⁵ *So Jehoiakim gave the silver and gold to Pharaoh; but he taxed the land to give money according to the command of Pharaoh; he exacted the silver and gold from the people of the land, from every one according to his assessment, to give it to Pharaoh Necho.*

³⁶ *Jehoiakim was twenty-five years old when he became king, and he reigned eleven years in Jerusalem. His mother's name was Zebudah the daughter of Pedaiah of Rumah.*

³⁷ *And he did evil in the sight of the LORD, according to all that his fathers had done.*

²⁴:¹ *In his days Nebuchadnezzar king of Babylon came up, and Jehoiakim became his vassal for three years. Then he turned and rebelled against him.*

² *And the LORD sent against him raiding bands of Chaldeans, bands of Syrians, bands of Moabites, and bands of the people of Ammon; He sent them against Judah to destroy it, according to the word of the LORD which He had spoken by His servants the prophets.*

³ *Surely at the commandment of the LORD this came upon Judah, to remove them from His sight because of the sins of Manasseh, according to all that he had done,*

⁴ *and also because of the innocent blood that he had shed; for he had filled Jerusalem with innocent blood, which the LORD would not pardon.*

⁵ *Now the rest of the acts of Jehoiakim, and all that he did, are they not written in the book of the chronicles of the kings of Judah?*

⁶ *So Jehoiakim rested with his fathers. Then Jehoiachin his son reigned in his place.*

# Exploring the Meaning

6) What kind of situation did Daniel and his friends leave behind in Judah? Why do you suppose Jehoiakim turned out to be so evil when his father Josiah had been such a godly man?

_____

_____

_____

_____

_____

7) Read Proverbs 4:23. What does it mean to "keep your heart with all diligence"? How does this command apply to what Daniel and his friends faced?

_____

_____

_____

_____

_____

8) Verse 8 says that Daniel "purposed in his heart . . . not to defile himself." The idea here is that he made up his mind or resolved not to compromise his principles. How does someone do this? What's involved in having firm purposes and enduring commitments? What's the downside in making these kinds of spiritual decisions? What's the upside?

_____

_____

_____

_____

_____

# Summing Up . . .

"The way out of the temptation is to endure it as a trial and never let it become a solicitation to evil. You have been wronged. You have been falsely accused. You have been maligned or treated unkindly or dealt with unjustly. So what? Accept it. Endure it with joy (James 1:2); that is the way of escape.

Usually we look for a quick and easy escape route. God's plan for us is different. He wants us to count it all joy, 'and let patience have its perfect work, that we may be perfect and complete, lacking nothing' (verse 4). God is using our trials to bring us to maturity."—*John MacArthur*

 ## *Reflecting on the Text*

9) The old song says it this way:

"Dare to be a Daniel, dare to stand alone;
Dare to have a purpose firm, dare to make it known."

Clearly, there is a difference between holding to a belief and entering into a conviction. A conviction is, in the words of one unknown writer, "nothing more than a belief with its boots on . . . ready to march, ready to fight, ready to die."

Do you agree? How would you distinguish the two? Which of the two words better describes your faith at this point in your life? Why?

_____

_____

_____

_____

_____

10) In 1 Samuel 2:30 God says, "those who honor Me I will honor." What are some practical ways you can honor God in the midst of a pagan culture that worships everything but the one true God?

_____

_____

_____

_____

_____

# Recording Your Thoughts

*For further study, see the following passages:*

Exodus 34:14–15

Ezra 1:1

2 Corinthians 6:14–18

Hebrews 11:24–26

2 Chronicles 16:9

Psalm 119:115

2 Timothy 2:20

2 Chronicles 36:5–8

Isaiah 46:1

Hebrews 7:26

# Nebuchadnezzar's Dreams

## Opening Thought

1) Think about the subject of dreams for a few minutes by pondering these questions:

Do you find that you dream often?
Are you able to remember your dreams when you wake in the morning?
What recurring dream(s) or nightmare(s) did you have when you were young?
What recurring dream(s) do you have now?
Why do you think some people have frequent (and strange!) dreams while others don't seem to dream much?

_____

_____

_____

_____

_____

_____

_____

_____

_____

_____

_____

# Background of the Passage

Chapter 2 reveals trouble in the royal palace of Babylon. King Nebuchadnezzar was having disturbing dreams that he could not understand. Summoning his assorted counselors, the king gave a disturbing command: Supply not only the meaning of the dreams but also their very content! Failure will result in death!

The magicians, astrologers, and sorcerers recognized the impossibility of this task, but Daniel immediately turned to His sovereign, all-knowing God in Whom all things are possible.

Following a time of prayer, "the secret was revealed to Daniel in a night vision" (verse 19). In short, Daniel revealed that God was giving Nebuchadnezzar a blueprint for world history. The dreams depicted five great, successive world empires that would rule over Israel-Babylon, Medo-Persia, Greece, Rome, and a revived Rome-followed by the final and eternal kingdom of Messiah.

Thus, on a theological level, chapter 2 is a prophetic outline that can aid in understanding God's sovereign activity in both human history and the yet-to-unfold events of the end times. On a personal and practical level, it is a wonderful reminder of the power of prayer in a believer's life.

# Bible Passage

Read 2:1–49, noting the key words and definitions to the right of the passage.

**Daniel 2:1–49**

1 Now in the second year of Nebuchadnezzar's reign, Nebuchadnezzar had dreams; and his spirit was so troubled that his sleep left him.

2 Then the king gave the command to call the magicians, the astrologers, the sorcerers, and the Chaldeans to tell the king his dreams. So they came and stood before the king.

3 And the king said to them, "I have had a dream, and my spirit is anxious to know the dream."

**second year** (v. 1)—The promotion of the four Hebrews after three years (1:5, 18) agrees with the year of promotion after the dream in the "second year."

**dreams** (v. 1)—During the time of revelation, God spoke through the interpretation of dreams that He induced.

**Chaldeans** (v. 2)—can refer to all people native to Chaldea (1:4; 3:8) or, as here, to a special class

⁴ *Then the Chaldeans spoke to the king in Aramaic, "O king, live forever! Tell your servants the dream, and we will give the interpretation."*

⁵ *The king answered and said to the Chaldeans, "My decision is firm: if you do not make known the dream to me, and its interpretation, you shall be cut in pieces, and your houses shall be made an ash heap.*

⁶ *"However, if you tell the dream and its interpretation, you shall receive from me gifts, rewards, and great honor. Therefore tell me the dream and its interpretation."*

⁷ *They answered again and said, "Let the king tell his servants the dream, and we will give its interpretation."*

⁸ *The king answered and said, "I know for certain that you would gain time, because you see that my decision is firm:*

⁹ *"if you do not make known the dream to me, there is only one decree for you! For you have agreed to speak lying and corrupt words before me till the time has changed. Therefore tell me the dream, and I shall know that you can give me its interpretation."*

¹⁰ *The Chaldeans answered the king, and said, "There is not a man on earth who can tell the king's matter; therefore no king, lord, or ruler has ever asked such things of any magician, astrologer, or Chaldean.*

¹¹ *"It is a difficult thing that the king requests, and there is no other who can tell it to the king except the gods, whose dwelling is not with flesh."*

¹² *For this reason the king was angry and very furious, and gave a command to destroy all the wise men of Babylon.*

¹³ *So the decree went out, and they began killing the wise men; and they sought Daniel and his companions, to kill them.*

¹⁴ *Then with counsel and wisdom Daniel answered Arioch, the captain of the king's guard, who had*

of soothsayers who taught Chaldean culture

**Aramaic** (v. 4)—the language to which Daniel suddenly switched midway through verse four and continued to write in until 7:28; its alphabet is similar to Hebrew but retains some distinctive differences; the abrupt switch probably has to do with the fact that the subject matter of 2:4b to 7:28 is largely focused on other nations and Aramaic was the language commonly used in governmental and trade relations

**My decision is firm** (v. 5)—The king shrewdly withheld the dream to test his experts; he was anxious for a genuine interpretation and feared deception if he were to reveal too much.

**Let the king tell** (v. 7)—These worldly men knew the impossibility of what the king was asking (see verse 11)-not only wisdom in understanding the meaning of the dream but omniscience in knowing what it was in the first place!

gone out to kill the wise men of Babylon;

15 he answered and said to Arioch the king's captain, "Why is the decree from the king so urgent?" Then Arioch made the decision known to Daniel.

16 So Daniel went in and asked the king to give him time, that he might tell the king the interpretation.

17 Then Daniel went to his house, and made the decision known to Hananiah, Mishael, and Azariah, his companions,

18 that they might seek mercies from the God of heaven concerning this secret, so that Daniel and his companions might not perish with the rest of the wise men of Babylon.

19 Then the secret was revealed to Daniel in a night vision. So Daniel blessed the God of heaven.

20 Daniel answered and said: "Blessed be the name of God forever and ever, For wisdom and might are His.

21 And He changes the times and the seasons; He removes kings and raises up kings; He gives wisdom to the wise And knowledge to those who have understanding.

22 He reveals deep and secret things; He knows what is in the darkness, And light dwells with Him.

23 "I thank You and praise You, O God of my fathers; You have given me wisdom and might, And have now made known to me what we asked of You, For You have made known to us the king's demand."

24 Therefore Daniel went to Arioch, whom the king had appointed to destroy the wise men of Babylon. He went and said thus to him: "Do not destroy the wise men of Babylon; take me before the king, and I will tell the king the interpretation."

25 Then Arioch quickly brought Daniel before the king, and said thus to him, "I have found a man of the captives of Judah, who will make known to the king the interpretation."

**Daniel . . . asked the king to give him time** (v. 16)—Daniel trusted God to grant him special revelation.

**that they might seek mercies** (v. 18)—Daniel solicited the prayer support of his Hebrew friends.

**the secret was revealed** (v. 19)—God graciously gave Daniel the dream and its meaning.

**Blessed be . . . God . . . for wisdom and might are His** (v. 20)—a summary of the theme of Daniel—God powerfully controls all things and is the source of all wisdom

<sup>26</sup> *The king answered and said to Daniel, whose name was Belteshazzar, "Are you able to make known to me the dream which I have seen, and its interpretation?"*

<sup>27</sup> *Daniel answered in the presence of the king, and said, "The secret which the king has demanded, the wise men, the astrologers, the magicians, and the soothsayers cannot declare to the king.*

<sup>28</sup> *"But there is a God in heaven who reveals secrets, and He has made known to King Nebuchadnezzar what will be in the latter days. Your dream, and the visions of your head upon your bed, were these:*

<sup>29</sup> *"As for you, O king, thoughts came to your mind while on your bed, about what would come to pass after this; and He who reveals secrets has made known to you what will be.*

<sup>30</sup> *"But as for me, this secret has not been revealed to me because I have more wisdom than anyone living, but for our sakes who make known the interpretation to the king, and that you may know the thoughts of your heart.*

<sup>31</sup> *"You, O king, were watching; and behold, a great image! This great image, whose splendor was excellent, stood before you; and its form was awesome.*

<sup>32</sup> *"This image's head was of fine gold, its chest and arms of silver, its belly and thighs of bronze,*

<sup>33</sup> *"its legs of iron, its feet partly of iron and partly of clay.*

<sup>34</sup> *"You watched while a stone was cut out without hands, which struck the image on its feet of iron and clay, and broke them in pieces.*

<sup>35</sup> *"Then the iron, the clay, the bronze, the silver, and the gold were crushed together, and became like chaff from the summer threshing floors; the wind carried them away so that no trace of them was found. And the stone that struck the image became a great mountain and filled the whole earth.*

**there is a God in heaven who reveals secrets** (v. 28)—in contrast to the impotent gods of the Babylonian astrologers and sorcerers

**not . . . because I have more wisdom than anyone living** (v. 30)—Daniel's humility is clearly revealed as he continually gave God the glory.

**this great image** (v. 31)—The parts of the statue represented the five successive empires—Babylon, Medo-Persia, Greece, Rome, and the later revived Rome—that would reign over Israel (in chapter 7 these same empires are represented by great beasts).

**stone . . . which struck the image** (v. 34)—representative of Christ at His second coming; he will destroy the fourth (Gentile) empire with great suddenness and establish His millennial kingdom, the ultimate empire

**36** "This is the dream. Now we will tell the interpretation of it before the king.

**37** "You, O king, are a king of kings. For the God of heaven has given you a kingdom, power, strength, and glory;

**38** "and wherever the children of men dwell, or the beasts of the field and the birds of the heaven, He has given them into your hand, and has made you ruler over them all-you are this head of gold.

**39** "But after you shall arise another kingdom inferior to yours; then another, a third kingdom of bronze, which shall rule over all the earth.

**40** "And the fourth kingdom shall be as strong as iron, inasmuch as iron breaks in pieces and shatters everything; and like iron that crushes, that kingdom will break in pieces and crush all the others.

**41** "Whereas you saw the feet and toes, partly of potter's clay and partly of iron, the kingdom shall be divided; yet the strength of the iron shall be in it, just as you saw the iron mixed with ceramic clay.

**42** "And as the toes of the feet were partly of iron and partly of clay, so the kingdom shall be partly strong and partly fragile.

**43** "As you saw iron mixed with ceramic clay, they will mingle with the seed of men; but they will not adhere to one another, just as iron does not mix with clay.

**44** "And in the days of these kings the God of heaven will set up a kingdom which shall never be destroyed; and the kingdom shall not be left to other people; it shall break in pieces and consume all these kingdoms, and it shall stand forever.

**45** "Inasmuch as you saw that the stone was cut out of the mountain without hands, and that it broke in pieces the iron, the bronze, the clay, the silver, and the gold—the great God has made known to the king what will come to pass after this. The dream is certain, and its interpretation is sure."

**inferior** (v. 39)—probably means "lower" (that is, "earthward") on the image of a man as Daniel guided Nebuchadnezzar's thoughts downward on the body from his own empire (the head) to the less glorious one that would follow it (that is, Medo-Persia)

**rule over all the earth** (v.39) —Alexander the Great became the ruler of the world, including Israel, from Europe to Egypt to India.

**strong as iron** (v. 40)—a fitting description of the Roman Empire, as its armies were noted for their iron armor

**toes** (v. 41)—These ten kings correspond to the ten horns of chapter 7 who will rule in the final time of the Gentile empire.

**clay and . . . iron** (vv. 41–43) —This revived Roman empire will have an iron-like strength for conquest, but the mixed-in clay shows that it will be vulnerable and flawed by human weakness.

**stand forever** (v. 44)—God's kingdom has a millennial phase and an eternal future; it is the final rule.

**mountain** (v. 45)—representative of God's all-transcending government

**without hands** (v. 45)— Messiah is not of human origin or power.

<sup>46</sup> *Then King Nebuchadnezzar fell on his face, prostrate before Daniel, and commanded that they should present an offering and incense to him.*

<sup>47</sup> *The king answered Daniel, and said, "Truly your God is the God of gods, the Lord of kings, and a revealer of secrets, since you could reveal this secret."*

<sup>48</sup> *Then the king promoted Daniel and gave him many great gifts; and he made him ruler over the whole province of Babylon, and chief administrator over all the wise men of Babylon.*

<sup>49</sup> *Also Daniel petitioned the king, and he set Shadrach, Meshach, and Abed-Nego over the affairs of the province of Babylon; but Daniel sat in the gate of the king.*

# *Understanding the Text*

2) Describe (or, if you're artistic, sketch) the image that Nebuchadnezzar saw in his dreams.

_____

_____

_____

_____

3) What steps or course of action did Daniel follow during this time of national and personal crisis?

_____

_____

_____

_____

4) What attributes of God are highlighted in this chapter?

_____

_____

_____

_____

## *Cross Reference*

Read in Genesis 40 about another believer with a divine gift for understanding dreams.

¹ *It came to pass after these things that the butler and the baker of the king of Egypt offended their lord, the king of Egypt.*

² *And Pharaoh was angry with his two officers, the chief butler and the chief baker.*

³ *So he put them in custody in the house of the captain of the guard, in the prison, the place where Joseph was confined.*

⁴ *And the captain of the guard charged Joseph with them, and he served them; so they were in custody for a while.*

⁵ *Then the butler and the baker of the king of Egypt, who were confined in the prison, had a dream, both of them, each man's dream in one night and each man's dream with its own interpretation.*

⁶ *And Joseph came in to them in the morning and looked at them, and saw that they were sad.*

⁷ *So he asked Pharaoh's officers who were with him in the custody of his lord's house, saying, "Why do you look so sad today?"*

⁸ *And they said to him, "We each have had a dream, and there is no interpreter of it." So Joseph said to them, "Do not interpretations belong to God? Tell them to me, please."*

⁹ *Then the chief butler told his dream to Joseph, and said to him, "Behold, in my dream a vine was before me,*

¹⁰ *"and in the vine were three branches; it was as though it budded, its blossoms shot forth, and its clusters brought forth ripe grapes.*

¹¹ *"Then Pharaoh's cup was in my hand; and I took the grapes and pressed them into Pharaoh's cup, and placed the cup in Pharaoh's hand."*

¹² *And Joseph said to him, "This is the interpretation of it: The three branches are three days.*

¹³ "Now within three days Pharaoh will lift up your head and restore you to your place, and you will put Pharaoh's cup in his hand according to the former manner, when you were his butler.

¹⁴ "But remember me when it is well with you, and please show kindness to me; make mention of me to Pharaoh, and get me out of this house.

¹⁵ "For indeed I was stolen away from the land of the Hebrews; and also I have done nothing here that they should put me into the dungeon."

¹⁶ When the chief baker saw that the interpretation was good, he said to Joseph, "I also was in my dream, and there were three white baskets on my head.

¹⁷ "In the uppermost basket were all kinds of baked goods for Pharaoh, and the birds ate them out of the basket on my head."

¹⁸ So Joseph answered and said, "This is the interpretation of it: The three baskets are three days.

¹⁹ "Within three days Pharaoh will lift off your head from you and hang you on a tree; and the birds will eat your flesh from you."

²⁰ Now it came to pass on the third day, which was Pharaoh's birthday, that he made a feast for all his servants; and he lifted up the head of the chief butler and of the chief baker among his servants.

²¹ Then he restored the chief butler to his butlership again, and he placed the cup in Pharaoh's hand.

²² But he hanged the chief baker, as Joseph had interpreted to them.

²³ Yet the chief butler did not remember Joseph, but forgot him.

# Exploring the Meaning

5) What similarities do you see between the situations faced by Daniel and Joseph? What differences are apparent? How are the two men alike?

_____

_____

_____

_____

6) In what way was Daniel honored by Nebuchadnezzar as a result of this incident? How did this affect Daniel? What is the danger in receiving human praise and reward?

_____

_____

_____

_____

7) Concerning the astrologers and charlatans who prey on weak people, have you ever wondered, "If they're really psychic, why do they have to ask you your name?"

In what ways are modern-day fortune tellers and psychics exactly like the "wise men" of Babylon depicted in chapter 2? Which is easier to fake: facts or the "interpretation" of those facts? Why do you think people accept such vague answers (and even pay to hear it)?

_____

_____

_____

_____

## Summing Up . . .

"Scripture . . . declares that the end times will be characterized by great concern for world unity, world government, world economics, and world religion (see 2; 7; Revelation 13; 17–18). The world is looking for stability and security and is ripe for the unifying role of a world leader who can stop wars and bring an end to political, economic, and social chaos—the role that one day will be filled by the antichrist.

"All of those signs that mark the end times are characteristic of our day. There can be no doubt that we live near the end of the age, and the concern of believers should be for what the Bible says rather than for what people say and for what God is doing rather than what people are doing."—*John MacArthur*

# *Reflecting on the Text*

8) Daniel made the king's "decision known to Hananiah, Mishael, and Azariah, his companions, that they might seek mercies from the God of heaven" (2:17–18). What's the lesson here for people today? What situation(s) do you need to make known to your Christian friends so that you can unite in prayer?

_____

_____

_____

_____

_____

9) After receiving an answer to his prayers, Daniel paused and gave thanks and honor to God. For what answer to prayer do you need to praise God today?

_____

_____

_____

_____

_____

10) Daniel used his position and privilege for kingdom purposes (see verses 46–49). In what practical ways can you use your gifts, abilities, position, training, and so forth to be a more prominent spokesman or representative for God?

_____

_____

_____

_____

_____

# Recording Your Thoughts

_____

_____

_____

_____

_____

_____

_____

_____

_____

_____

_____

_____

_____

_____

_____

_____

_____

_____

_____

_____

_____

_____

## For further study, see the following passages:

| | | |
|---|---|---|
| Genesis 40:8 | Genesis 41:1 | Genesis 41:16 |
| Exodus 8:16–19 | Psalm 47:8 | Psalm 118:22–23 |
| Isaiah 28:16 | Daniel 7:13–14 | Luke 20:18 |
| Romans 9:33 | 1 Peter 2:6 | Revelation 13:4–5 |
| Revelation 17:9 | | |

# The Fiery Furnace

## *Opening Thought*

1) What are your favorite miracle stories from the Bible? Why?

_____

_____

_____

_____

_____

_____

_____

_____

_____

_____

_____

_____

_____

_____

_____

_____

_____

_____

_____

_____

# Background of the Passage

Chapter 3 is one of the best loved of all Bible stories. It is the story known simply as the "Hebrew children and the fiery furnace."

The facts are familiar to most. Despite Nebuchadnezzar's previous claim that Daniel's God "is the God of gods [and] the Lord of kings" (2:47), he reverted to heinous idolatry, setting up a giant golden image and demanding that his subjects worship it alone.

When it was reported that Shadrach, Meshach, and Abednego (that is, the Hebrew captives Hananiah, Mishael, and Azariah mentioned in 1:6–7 and 2:17) were violating the new royal decree, Nebuchadnezzar became outraged and summoned them at once. They were given a final chance to obey the idolatrous edict; but when the young Jewish men steadfastly refused to comply, it was ordered that they be cast into "the midst of a burning fiery furnace" (verse 15).

Ironically, the great heat of the furnace killed the executioners but not the faithful Hebrews. God miraculously delivered them, prompting Nebuchadnezzar to once again note the uniqueness and supremacy of the God of the Hebrews.

# Bible Passage

Read 3:1–30, noting the key words and definitions to the right of the passage.

### Daniel 3:1–30

1 *Nebuchadnezzar the king made an image of gold, whose height was sixty cubits and its width six cubits. He set it up in the plain of Dura, in the province of Babylon.*

2 *And King Nebuchadnezzar sent word to gather together the satraps, the administrators, the governors, the counselors, the treasurers, the judges, the magistrates, and all the officials of the provinces, to come to the dedication of the image which King Nebuchadnezzar had set up.*

**image of gold** (v. 1)—This ninety-foot-tall statue, overlaid with gold (it was probably not solid gold) likely was a glorious representation of Nebuchadnezzar ("image" typically refers to a human form); he may have gotten the idea from the dreams of chapter 2 in which he saw himself as a head of gold.

**satraps . . . officials** (v. 2)—assorted government leaders and dignitaries (probable meanings: satraps = regional leaders; admin-

³ So the satraps, the administrators, the governors, the counselors, the treasurers, the judges, the magistrates, and all the officials of the provinces gathered together for the dedication of the image that King Nebuchadnezzar had set up; and they stood before the image that Nebuchadnezzar had set up.

⁴ Then a herald cried aloud: "To you it is commanded, O peoples, nations, and languages,

⁵ "that at the time you hear the sound of the horn, flute, harp, lyre, and psaltery, in symphony with all kinds of music, you shall fall down and worship the gold image that King Nebuchadnezzar has set up;

⁶ "and whoever does not fall down and worship shall be cast immediately into the midst of a burning fiery furnace."

⁷ So at that time, when all the people heard the sound of the horn, flute, harp, and lyre, in symphony with all kinds of music, all the people, nations, and languages fell down and worshiped the gold image which King Nebuchadnezzar had set up.

⁸ Therefore at that time certain Chaldeans came forward and accused the Jews.

⁹ They spoke and said to King Nebuchadnezzar, "O king, live forever!

¹⁰ "You, O king, have made a decree that everyone who hears the sound of the horn, flute, harp, lyre, and psaltery, in symphony with all kinds of music, shall fall down and worship the gold image;

¹¹ "and whoever does not fall down and worship shall be cast into the midst of a burning fiery furnace.

¹² "There are certain Jews whom you have set over the affairs of the province of Babylon: Shadrach, Meshach, and Abed-Nego; these men, O king, have not paid due regard to you. They do not

istrators = military chiefs; counselors = lawyers; officials = other civic leaders)

**lyre** (v. 5)—a harp, possibly square or rectangular with strings to pluck with a plectrum (that is, pick), yielding high tones

**psaltery** (v. 5)—an instrument plucked with the fingers resulting in deep tones

**furnace** (v. 6)—probably a kiln fueled by charcoal; ancient ruins have shown some to be vertical tunnels open only at the top with a dome supported by columns

**certain Chaldeans** (v. 8)—likely priests of Bel-Merodach who were envious of the gifts and positions enjoyed by these young Jewish men

**They do not . . . worship the gold image** (v. 12)—The Hebrews' allegiance to Yahweh was unmistakable.

**these men** (v. 12)—Daniel is not mentioned, though there is no reason to suspect that he indulged in idolatry.

serve your gods or worship the gold image which you have set up."

13 Then Nebuchadnezzar, in rage and fury, gave the command to bring Shadrach, Meshach, and Abed-Nego. So they brought these men before the king.

14 Nebuchadnezzar spoke, saying to them, "Is it true, Shadrach, Meshach, and Abed-Nego, that you do not serve my gods or worship the gold image which I have set up?

15 "Now if you are ready at the time you hear the sound of the horn, flute, harp, lyre, and psaltery, in symphony with all kinds of music, and you fall down and worship the image which I have made, good! But if you do not worship, you shall be cast immediately into the midst of a burning fiery furnace. And who is the god who will deliver you from my hands?"

16 Shadrach, Meshach, and Abed-Nego answered and said to the king, "O Nebuchadnezzar, we have no need to answer you in this matter.

17 "If that is the case, our God whom we serve is able to deliver us from the burning fiery furnace, and He will deliver us from your hand, O king.

18 "But if not, let it be known to you, O king, that we do not serve your gods, nor will we worship the gold image which you have set up."

19 Then Nebuchadnezzar was full of fury, and the expression on his face changed toward Shadrach, Meshach, and Abed-Nego. He spoke and commanded that they heat the furnace seven times more than it was usually heated.

20 And he commanded certain mighty men of valor who were in his army to bind Shadrach, Meshach, and Abed-Nego, and cast them into the burning fiery furnace.

22 Then these men were bound in their coats, their trousers, their turbans, and their other garments, and were cast into the midst of the burning fiery furnace.

**who is the god?** (v. 15)—The king's challenge would return to embarrass him; the true God was able to deliver just as he was able to reveal a secret dream and its meaning.

**we have no need to answer** (v. 16)—No disrespect was meant; the men felt no obligation to make a defense or apology for their actions; there was nothing to discuss.

**But if not** (v. 18)—a classic statement of trust and the commitment to faithfulness regardless of the cost

**seven times more** (v. 19)—not a literal requirement, as this would have been difficult to measure, but perhaps a command for the kiln to be fired up for seven times as long or to be stoked with seven times as much fuel

**took up** (v. 22)—This indicates some sort of ramp from which the men were thrown down into the furnace. The soldiers/executioners involved were themselves incinerated by the intense heat.

22 *Therefore, because the king's command was urgent, and the furnace exceedingly hot, the flame of the fire killed those men who took up Shadrach, Meshach, and Abed-Nego.*

23 *And these three men, Shadrach, Meshach, and Abed-Nego, fell down bound into the midst of the burning fiery furnace.*

24 *Then King Nebuchadnezzar was astonished; and he rose in haste and spoke, saying to his counselors, "Did we not cast three men bound into the midst of the fire?" They answered and said to the king, "True, O king."*

25 *"Look!" he answered, "I see four men loose, walking in the midst of the fire; and they are not hurt, and the form of the fourth is like the Son of God."*

26 *Then Nebuchadnezzar went near the mouth of the burning fiery furnace and spoke, saying, "Shadrach, Meshach, and Abed-Nego, servants of the Most High God, come out, and come here." Then Shadrach, Meshach, and Abed-Nego came from the midst of the fire.*

27 *And the satraps, administrators, governors, and the king's counselors gathered together, and they saw these men on whose bodies the fire had no power; the hair of their head was not singed nor were their garments affected, and the smell of fire was not on them.*

28 *Nebuchadnezzar spoke, saying, "Blessed be the God of Shadrach, Meshach, and Abed-Nego, who sent His Angel and delivered His servants who trusted in Him, and they have frustrated the king's word, and yielded their bodies, that they should not serve nor worship any god except their own God!*

29 *"Therefore I make a decree that any people, nation, or language which speaks anything amiss against the God of Shadrach, Meshach, and Abed-Nego shall be cut in pieces, and their houses shall be made an ash heap; because there is no other God who can deliver like this."*

**fell down** (v. 23)—down a shaft into the dome-like bottom, on top of the fuel

**four men loose** (v. 25)—The king recognized the fourth person as divine; he called him a son of the gods (a common pagan phrase for supernatural beings) and an angel. This may actually have been Jesus Christ in His pre-incarnate state.

**the fire had no power** (v. 27)—God supernaturally (that is, miraculously) overrode natural law so that their clothes did not even have a smoky smell.

³⁰ *Then the king promoted Shadrach, Meshach, and*
*Abed-Nego in the province of Babylon.*

## Understanding the Text

2) Describe the spectacle of 3:1–7. What was going on? What do you think precipitated this turn of events (especially in light of 2:47)?

_____

_____

_____

_____

3) How did the king discover the unwillingness of the Hebrews to worship his giant idol? How did they respond when confronted?

_____

_____

_____

_____

4) What happened when the execution was carried out? What was the final outcome of this episode?

_____

_____

_____

_____

_____

# Cross Reference

Read the following passage from Acts 4:

⁵ *And it came to pass, on the next day, that their rulers, elders, and scribes,*

⁶ *as well as Annas the high priest, Caiaphas, John, and Alexander, and as many as were of the family of the high priest, were gathered together at Jerusalem.*

⁷ *And when they had set them in the midst, they asked, "By what power or by what name have you done this?"*

⁸ *Then Peter, filled with the Holy Spirit, said to them, "Rulers of the people and elders of Israel:*

⁹ *"If we this day are judged for a good deed done to a helpless man, by what means he has been made well,*

¹⁰ *"let it be known to you all, and to all the people of Israel, that by the name of Jesus Christ of Nazareth, whom you crucified, whom God raised from the dead, by Him this man stands here before you whole.*

¹¹ *"This is the 'stone which was rejected by you builders, which has become the chief cornerstone.'*

¹² *"Nor is there salvation in any other, for there is no other name under heaven given among men by which we must be saved."*

¹³ *Now when they saw the boldness of Peter and John, and perceived that they were uneducated and untrained men, they marveled. And they realized that they had been with Jesus.*

¹⁴ *And seeing the man who had been healed standing with them, they could say nothing against it.*

¹⁵ *But when they had commanded them to go aside out of the council, they conferred among themselves,*

¹⁶ *saying, "What shall we do to these men? For, indeed, that a notable miracle has been done through them is evident to all who dwell in Jerusalem, and we cannot deny it.*

¹⁷ *"But so that it spreads no further among the people, let us severely threaten them, that from now on they speak to no man in this name."*

¹⁸ *And they called them and commanded them not to speak at all nor teach in the name of Jesus.*

¹⁹ *But Peter and John answered and said to them, "Whether it is right in the sight of God to listen to you more than to God, you judge.*

²⁰ *"For we cannot but speak the things which we have seen and heard."*

# Exploring the Meaning

5) How is the situation in Acts 4 similar to the events of chapter 3? What principles are at stake?

_____

_____

_____

_____

_____

6) Read Romans 13. If Christians are to obey their civil leaders, how do we explain the behavior of the Hebrew men in chapter 3 and the apostles in Acts 4? When does God approve of civil disobedience?

_____

_____

_____

_____

_____

_____

(verses to consider: Matthew 22:21; Acts 5:29; Titus 3:1; 1 Peter 2:13–14)

7) Who was the fourth person in the furnace? How do you know this?

_____

_____

_____

_____

_____

# Summing Up . . .

"[This] is faith at its highest-the absolute conviction that God is able, coupled with humble submission to His sovereignty in the exercise of His power."
—*John MacArthur*

# Reflecting on the Text

8) Where are you being pressured to compromise your faith?

_____

_____

_____

_____

_____

> *Complete this paraphrase of 3:17–18: "God, whom I serve, is able to _____. But if not, let it be known that I will _____ and I will not _____."*

9) An idol is anything that takes the place of God in a person's life. Devoting the best of our attention, affection, energy, time, and resources to something other than God makes that thing or person an idol.

Most people are too sophisticated for idols in statue form, but what things have a tendency to become more valuable to you than God?

_____

_____

_____

_____

10) What people do you know who have risked everything by standing for Christ? Pray for them. Consider writing them a note of encouragement and appreciation this week.

_____

_____

_____

_____

_____

_____

## *Recording Your Thoughts*

_____

_____

_____

_____

_____

_____

_____

_____

_____

_____

_____

_____

## *For further study, see the following passages:*

| | | |
|---|---|---|
| Leviticus 26:18–28 | Joshua 5:13–15 | Judges 6:11 |
| Proverbs 6:31 | Isaiah 43:1–2 | |

# The Humiliation of a Proud King

## *Opening Thought*

1) Power corrupts; absolute power corrupts absolutely. (Lord Acton) What do you think that statement means?

_____

_____

_____

_____

2) As you think back over your lifetime, what government leaders and elected officials would you classify as genuine public servants? Is your list a long one? Why?

_____

_____

_____

_____

3) Why is it so common for those with immense God-given talent and those who are able to accomplish great things to forget the One ultimately responsible for their success?

_____

_____

_____

_____

# Background of the Passage

Chapter 4 continues the fascinating record of King Nebuchadnezzar. After conquering Judah and exiling its most gifted young people to Babylon (chapter 1), Nebuchadnezzar began having disturbing dreams (chapter 2) that could only be interpreted by Daniel, one of his captive Jews. The dreams revealed the sovereignty of God over the nations and future world events.

But Nebuchadnezzar was slow to acknowledge the authority and supremacy of Yahweh, for chapter 3 records his gross idolatry and the refusal of his Hebrew subjects to pay homage to the idol he had erected. Even a miraculous deliverance by the one true God produced only a token expression of praise (3:28–29) from Nebuchadnezzar's lips.

Next, chapter 4 gives the record of God's very painful and personal humiliation of Nebuchadnezzar. Because of his stubborn pride, this world leader was reduced to animal status ("his body was wet with the dew of heaven till his hair had grown like eagles' [feathers] and his nails like birds' [claws]"). In this state he remained until at last in humility he lifted his eyes to heaven (verse 34).

The message of chapter 4 is clear: God is preeminent, and He will not give His glory to another (Isaiah 48:11).

# Bible Passage

Read 4:1–37, noting the key words and definitions to the right of the passage.

### Daniel 4:1–37

¹ *Nebuchadnezzar the king, To all peoples, nations, and languages that dwell in all the earth: Peace be multiplied to you.*

² *I thought it good to declare the signs and wonders that the Most High God has worked for me.*

³ *How great are His signs, And how mighty His*

**that the Most High God has worked for me** (v. 2)— Nebuchadnezzar's praise of God here and at the end of the chapter is the theme that brackets the experience of verses 4–34; his reason for converting to Yahweh worship is explained in heart of the passage.

wonders! His kingdom is an everlasting kingdom, And His dominion is from generation to generation.

4 I, Nebuchadnezzar, was at rest in my house, and flourishing in my palace.

5 I saw a dream which made me afraid, and the thoughts on my bed and the visions of my head troubled me.

6 Therefore I issued a decree to bring in all the wise men of Babylon before me, that they might make known to me the interpretation of the dream.

7 Then the magicians, the astrologers, the Chaldeans, and the soothsayers came in, and I told them the dream; but they did not make known to me its interpretation.

8 But at last Daniel came before me (his name is Belteshazzar, according to the name of my god; in him is the Spirit of the Holy God), and I told the dream before him, saying:

9 "Belteshazzar, chief of the magicians, because I know that the Spirit of the Holy God is in you, and no secret troubles you, explain to me the visions of my dream that I have seen, and its interpretation.

10 These were the visions of my head while on my bed: I was looking, and behold, A tree in the midst of the earth, And its height was great.

11 The tree grew and became strong; Its height reached to the heavens, And it could be seen to the ends of all the earth.

12 Its leaves were lovely, Its fruit abundant, And in it was food for all. The beasts of the field found shade under it, The birds of the heavens dwelt in its branches, And all flesh was fed from it.

13 "I saw in the visions of my head while on my bed, and there was a watcher, a holy one, coming down from heaven.

14 He cried aloud and said thus: 'Chop down the tree and cut off its branches, Strip off its leaves and scatter its fruit. Let the beasts get out from under it, And the birds from its branches.

**wise men of Babylon** (v. 6)— The king gave them another try, and they were again unable to interpret his dreams.

**at last Daniel came** (v. 8)— Enabled by God, Daniel alone interpreted the tree vision (verse 10).

**my god** (v. 8)—At the beginning of the story, Nebuchadnezzar depicted himself as a worshiper of Bel-Merodach.

**chief of the magicians** (v. 9)— a title the pagans gave him

**Spirit** (v. 9)—The meaning here and in verse 18 (as well as 5:11, 14) is rightly translated as, "the Spirit of the holy God." The claim by some that this means "a spirit of the holy gods" is unlikely since no pagan worshipers claimed purity or holiness for their deities.

**a tree** (v. 10)—a picture of Nebuchadnezzar after 605 B.C.

**beasts . . . birds** (v. 12)—representative of people under Nebuchadnezzar's rule

**a watcher, a holy one** (v. 13) —an angel (see verse 23), a servant of God, who controlled a nation's rise or fall (see 10:13)

**Chop down the tree** (v. 14)— a reference to God's coming judgment on Nebuchadnezzar

15 *Nevertheless leave the stump and roots in the earth, Bound with a band of iron and bronze, In the tender grass of the field. Let it be wet with the dew of heaven, And let him graze with the beasts On the grass of the earth.*

16 *Let his heart be changed from that of a man, Let him be given the heart of a beast, And let seven times pass over him.*

17 *'This decision is by the decree of the watchers, And the sentence by the word of the holy ones, In order that the living may know That the Most High rules in the kingdom of men, Gives it to whomever He will, And sets over it the lowest of men.'*

18 *"This dream I, King Nebuchadnezzar, have seen. Now you, Belteshazzar, declare its interpretation, since all the wise men of my kingdom are not able to make known to me the interpretation; but you are able, for the Spirit of the Holy God is in you."*

19 *Then Daniel, whose name was Belteshazzar, was astonished for a time, and his thoughts troubled him. So the king spoke, and said, "Belteshazzar, do not let the dream or its interpretation trouble you." Belteshazzar answered and said, "My lord, may the dream concern those who hate you, and its interpretation concern your enemies!*

20 *The tree that you saw, which grew and became strong, whose height reached to the heavens and which could be seen by all the earth,*

21 *whose leaves were lovely and its fruit abundant, in which was food for all, under which the beasts of the field dwelt, and in whose branches the birds of the heaven had their home-*

22 *it is you, O king, who have grown and become strong; for your greatness has grown and reaches to the heavens, and your dominion to the end of the earth.*

23 *And inasmuch as the king saw a watcher, a holy one, coming down from heaven and saying,*

**stump** (v. 15)—The basis (nucleus) of the kingdom, still in existence in verse 26 will sprout later as in nature. The band is a guarantee that God will protect what remains intact and preserve the king's rule.

**heart of a beast** (v. 16)—some form of the disease called lycanthropy, in which a person thinks he is an animal and acts like it

**seven times** (v. 16)—probably years are meant (see 7:25), not "months," which is used in verse 29

**astonished** (v. 19)—Daniel's compassionate alarm over the coming calamity

'Chop down the tree and destroy it, but leave its stump and roots in the earth, bound with a band of iron and bronze in the tender grass of the field; let it be wet with the dew of heaven, and let him graze with the beasts of the field, till seven times pass over him';

24 this is the interpretation, O king, and this is the decree of the Most High, which has come upon my lord the king:

25 They shall drive you from men, your dwelling shall be with the beasts of the field, and they shall make you eat grass like oxen. They shall wet you with the dew of heaven, and seven times shall pass over you, till you know that the Most High rules in the kingdom of men, and gives it to whomever He chooses.

26 And inasmuch as they gave the command to leave the stump and roots of the tree, your kingdom shall be assured to you, after you come to know that Heaven rules.

27 Therefore, O king, let my advice be acceptable to you; break off your sins by being righteous, and your iniquities by showing mercy to the poor. Perhaps there may be a lengthening of your prosperity."

28 All this came upon King Nebuchadnezzar.

29 At the end of the twelve months he was walking about the royal palace of Babylon.

30 The king spoke, saying, "Is not this great Babylon, that I have built for a royal dwelling by my mighty power and for the honor of my majesty?"

31 While the word was still in the king's mouth, a voice fell from heaven: "King Nebuchadnezzar, to you it is spoken: the kingdom has departed from you!

32 And they shall drive you from men, and your dwelling shall be with the beasts of the field. They shall make you eat grass like oxen; and seven times shall pass over you, until you know

**Heaven rules** (v. 26)—God is synonymous with His abode.

**break off your sins** (v. 27)—Daniel called for a recognition of sin and repentance; he was not presenting a works salvation but treating the issue of sin exactly as Jesus always did. But the king failed to repent at this point.

**I have built** (v. 30)—Nebuchadnezzar was noted for his building projects, such as a four-hundred-foot high mountain terraced with flowing water and hanging gardens for his wife (one of the seven wonders of the ancient world) as a place for cool refreshment; for such pride, judgment fell (verses 31–33).

**lifted my eyes** (v. 34)—God's grace enables a person to do this.

*that the Most High rules in the kingdom of men, and gives it to whomever He chooses."*

³³ *That very hour the word was fulfilled concerning Nebuchadnezzar; he was driven from men and ate grass like oxen; his body was wet with the dew of heaven till his hair had grown like eagles' feathers and his nails like birds' claws.*

³⁴ *And at the end of the time I, Nebuchadnezzar, lifted my eyes to heaven, and my understanding returned to me; and I blessed the Most High and praised and honored Him who lives forever: For His dominion is an everlasting dominion, And His kingdom is from generation to generation.*

³⁵ *All the inhabitants of the earth are reputed as nothing; He does according to His will in the army of heaven And among the inhabitants of the earth. No one can restrain His hand Or say to Him, "What have You done?"*

³⁶ *At the same time my reason returned to me, and for the glory of my kingdom, my honor and splendor returned to me. My counselors and nobles resorted to me, I was restored to my kingdom, and excellent majesty was added to me.*

³⁷ *Now I, Nebuchadnezzar, praise and extol and honor the King of heaven, all of whose works are truth, and His ways justice. And those who walk in pride He is able to put down.*

# *Understanding the Text*

4) Why was Nebuchadnezzar troubled (verse 5)? What did he do as a result of being so disturbed? What was his opinion of Daniel?

_____

_____

_____

_____

_____

5) Once summoned, what did Daniel tell the king? Was this advice heeded or not? How do you know?

_____

_____

_____

_____

6) What was the final outcome of this whole experience? Did Nebuchadnezzar change?

_____

_____

_____

_____

_____

# Cross Reference

Read the following passage from Acts 12:

[20] *Now Herod had been very angry with the people of Tyre and Sidon; but they came to him with one accord, and having made Blastus the king's personal aide their friend, they asked for peace, because their country was supplied with food by the king's country.*

[21] *So on a set day Herod, arrayed in royal apparel, sat on his throne and gave an oration to them.*

[22] *And the people kept shouting, "The voice of a god and not of a man!"*

[23] *Then immediately an angel of the Lord struck him, because he did not give glory to God. And he was eaten by worms and died.*

# *Exploring the Meaning*

7) In what ways was Herod (Acts 12:20–23) similar to Nebuchadnezzar? Why is it that power seems to so often go hand in hand with pride? How did the outcomes of the men differ?

_____

_____

_____

_____

_____

_____

8) Read Proverbs 3:34 and 1 Samuel 2:30. What light do these passages shed on the events of chapter 4?

_____

_____

_____

_____

_____

9) Do you think Daniel was perhaps a bit anxious when he spoke the words of 4:27? Why or why not? What are the potential risks for speaking hard truths to hard hearts?

_____

_____

_____

_____

_____

(verses to consider: 2 Samuel 12:1–13; Matthew 14:3–4)

# Summing Up . . .

"Pride is the supreme temptation from Satan because pride is at the heart of his own evil nature. Consequently, Satan makes sure that the Christian is never entirely free from the temptation of pride. We will always be in a battle with pride until the Lord takes us to be with Himself. Our only protection against pride, and our only source of humility, is a proper view of God. Pride is the sin of competing with God, and humility is the virtue of submitting to His supreme glory. . . . Humility is an ingredient of all spiritual blessing . . . [it] is behind every harmonious human relationship, every spiritual success, and every moment of joyous fellowship with the Lord." — *John MacArthur*

# Reflecting on the Text

10) In what areas of your life (for example, career, accomplishments, financial status, natural abilities, and so forth) are you, like Nebuchadnezzar, failing to acknowledge God's authority and, instead, exalting yourself?

_____

_____

_____

_____

_____

_____

11) What do you need to do? How does one become a humble person?

_____

_____

_____

_____

_____

_____

12) What lesson(s) can you learn from Daniel's willingness to call on King Nebuchadnezzar (the most powerful man in the world at that time) to repent?

_____

_____

_____

_____

13) When has God humbled you? What happened? What did you learn? How does a person remain humble?

_____

_____

_____

_____

_____

## *Recording Your Thoughts*

_____

_____

_____

_____

_____

_____

## *For further study, see the following passages:*

| | | |
|---|---|---|
| Genesis 18 | Joshua 24:19 | Isaiah 37 |
| Isaiah 55:7 | Daniel 2:2–13 | Daniel 10:13 |
| Matthew 19:16–23 | John 6:44, 65 | Romans 11:33 |
| Revelation 16 | | |

# Belshazzar's Fall

## Opening Thought

1) What are some of the most outrageous, most public challenges to the reality and holiness of God that you've witnessed in recent years? Is this kind of anti-God sentiment and behavior increasing and becoming more brazen, or has sacrilegious activity always been this extreme?

_____

_____

_____

_____

_____

_____

_____

_____

_____

_____

_____

_____

_____

_____

_____

_____

# Background of the Passage

Judah, because of her stubborn sinfulness, had been taken into captivity by the Babylonians (chapter 1). Although this turn of events (an evil nation being used as an instrument of judgment against the wayward people of God) was troubling and confusing to many Israelites (see Habakkuk), it only demonstrated God's sovereignty. Psalm 46:10 declares, "Be still, and know that I [am] God; I will be exalted among the nations, I will be exalted in the earth!"

Thus, in the perfect and unstoppable plan of God, the day of reckoning eventually arrived for godless Babylon too. Chapter 5 reveals the debauchery and demise of the empire under Belshazzar. Just as had happened with Egypt during the time of Moses, God brought low an arrogant man and a proud nation, and in the process He brought glory to Himself through a quiet but powerful servant.

The end of chapter 5 witnesses the appearance of the Medo-Persians on the stage of world history. At that time, Daniel, a model of humility and faithfulness during an already lengthy career was in position to have an international impact.

# Bible Passage

Read 5:1–31, noting the key words and definitions to the right of the passage.

## Daniel 5:1–31

1 *Belshazzar the king made a great feast for a thousand of his lords, and drank wine in the presence of the thousand.*

2 *While he tasted the wine, Belshazzar gave the command to bring the gold and silver vessels which his father Nebuchadnezzar had taken from the temple which had been in Jerusalem, that the king and his lords, his wives, and his concubines might drink from them.*

**Belshazzar** (v. 1)—These events occurred in 539 B.C., over two decades after his father Nebuchadnezzar's death (about 563 B.C.) and just prior to his being conquered by the Medo-Persians. His name means "Bel, protect the king."

**vessels** (v. 2)—This celebration was an attempt to boost morale, since at the time of the feast the Medo-Persian army was advancing against the Babylonians.

³ Then they brought the gold vessels that had been taken from the temple of the house of God which had been in Jerusalem; and the king and his lords, his wives, and his concubines drank from them.

⁴ They drank wine, and praised the gods of gold and silver, bronze and iron, wood and stone.

⁵ In the same hour the fingers of a man's hand appeared and wrote opposite the lampstand on the plaster of the wall of the king's palace; and the king saw the part of the hand that wrote.

⁶ Then the king's countenance changed, and his thoughts troubled him, so that the joints of his hips were loosened and his knees knocked against each other.

⁷ The king cried aloud to bring in the astrologers, the Chaldeans, and the soothsayers. The king spoke, saying to the wise men of Babylon, "Whoever reads this writing, and tells me its interpretation, shall be clothed with purple and have a chain of gold around his neck; and he shall be the third ruler in the kingdom."

⁸ Now all the king's wise men came, but they could not read the writing, or make known to the king its interpretation.

⁹ Then King Belshazzar was greatly troubled, his countenance was changed, and his lords were astonished.

¹⁰ The queen, because of the words of the king and his lords, came to the banquet hall. The queen spoke, saying, "O king, live forever! Do not let your thoughts trouble you, nor let your countenance change.

¹¹ "There is a man in your kingdom in whom is the Spirit of the Holy God. And in the days of your father, light and understanding and wisdom, like the wisdom of the gods, were found in him; and King Nebuchadnezzar your father—your father the king—made him chief of the magicians, astrologers, Chaldeans, and soothsayers.

**praised the gods of gold and silver** (v. 4)—an exercise in which these deities were called upon for help

**man's hand** (v. 5)—Babylonian hands had taken God's vessels (notice the two mentions) and held them in contempt to dishonor and challenge Him. At this time, the Hand that controls all things, and that none can restrain, challenged the Babylonians.

**they could not** (v. 8)—Without God's help, the Babylonian experts again were unable to interpret these supernatural signs.

**The queen spoke** (v. 10)—She may have been a surviving wife or daughter of Nebuchadnezzar. If the latter, she would have been a wife of Nabonidus, co-ruler with Belshazzar.

**There is a man** (v. 11)—Like her father, she had confidence in Daniel.

<sup>12</sup> *"Inasmuch as an excellent spirit, knowledge, understanding, interpreting dreams, solving riddles, and explaining enigmas were found in this Daniel, whom the king named Belteshazzar, now let Daniel be called, and he will give the interpretation."*

<sup>13</sup> *Then Daniel was brought in before the king. The king spoke, and said to Daniel, "Are you that Daniel who is one of the captives from Judah, whom my father the king brought from Judah?*

<sup>14</sup> *"I have heard of you, that the Spirit of God is in you, and that light and understanding and excellent wisdom are found in you.*

<sup>15</sup> *"Now the wise men, the astrologers, have been brought in before me, that they should read this writing and make known to me its interpretation, but they could not give the interpretation of the thing.*

<sup>16</sup> *"And I have heard of you, that you can give interpretations and explain enigmas. Now if you can read the writing and make known to me its interpretation, you shall be clothed with purple and have a chain of gold around your neck, and shall be the third ruler in the kingdom."*

<sup>17</sup> *Then Daniel answered, and said before the king, "Let your gifts be for yourself, and give your rewards to another; yet I will read the writing to the king, and make known to him the interpretation.*

<sup>18</sup> *"O king, the Most High God gave Nebuchadnezzar your father a kingdom and majesty, glory and honor.*

<sup>19</sup> *"And because of the majesty that He gave him, all peoples, nations, and languages trembled and feared before him. Whomever he wished, he executed; whomever he wished, he kept alive; whomever he wished, he set up; and whomever he wished, he put down.*

<sup>20</sup> *"But when his heart was lifted up, and his spirit*

**explaining enigmas** (v. 12)—literally, "untying knots" (that is, difficult conundrums)

**the third ruler** (v. 16)—The trio included Daniel, along with Belshazzar, Nebuchadnezzar's grandson (ruled 553-539 B.C.), and Nabonidus (ruled 556-539 B.C.). The prizes were never rewarded since the city was conquered that very night.

was hardened in pride, he was deposed from his kingly throne, and they took his glory from him.

21 *"Then he was driven from the sons of men, his heart was made like the beasts, and his dwelling was with the wild donkeys. They fed him with grass like oxen, and his body was wet with the dew of heaven, till he knew that the Most High God rules in the kingdom of men, and appoints over it whomever He chooses.*

22 *"But you his son, Belshazzar, have not humbled your heart, although you knew all this.*

23 *"And you have lifted yourself up against the Lord of heaven. They have brought the vessels of His house before you, and you and your lords, your wives and your concubines, have drunk wine from them. And you have praised the gods of silver and gold, bronze and iron, wood and stone, which do not see or hear or know; and the God who holds your breath in His hand and owns all your ways, you have not glorified.*

24 *"Then the fingers of the hand were sent from Him, and this writing was written.*

25 *"And this is the inscription that was written: MENE, MENE, TEKEL, UPHARSIN.*

26 *"This is the interpretation of each word. MENE: God has numbered your kingdom, and finished it;*

27 *"TEKEL: You have been weighed in the balances, and found wanting;*

28 *"PERES: Your kingdom has been divided, and given to the Medes and Persians."*

29 *Then Belshazzar gave the command, and they clothed Daniel with purple and put a chain of gold around his neck, and made a proclamation concerning him that he should be the third ruler in the kingdom.*

30 *That very night Belshazzar, king of the Chaldeans, was slain.*

31 *And Darius the Mede received the kingdom, being about sixty-two years old.*

**MENE, MENE** (v. 25)—This means "counted" or "appointed" and is doubled for stronger emphasis.

**TEKEL** (v. 25)—This means "weighed" or "assessed" by the God who weighs actions.

**UPHARSIN** (v. 25)—The "u" prefix means "and," and *pharsin* is the plural of *peres*, which means "divided," that is, to the Medes and Persians.

*That very night* (v. 30)—One ancient account alleged that Persia's General Ugbaru had troops dig a trench to divert and thus lower the waters of the Euphrates River; since the river flowed through the city of Babylon, the lowered water enabled besiegers to unexpectedly invade via the waterway under the thick walls and reach the palace before the city was aware. The end came quickly on October 16, 539 B.C.

*Darius the Mede* (v. 31)—possibly not a name but a title for Cyrus, who with his army entered Babylon on Oct. 29, 539 B.C.; Darius is used in inscriptions for at least 5 other Persian rulers

*received the kingdom* (v. 31) —As prophesied, Babylon met God's judgment.

# *Understanding the Text*

2) Describe the mood at Belshazzar's feast. What was happening in the palace? What about outside the palace? Of what prideful act was Belshazzar guilty?

_____

_____

_____

_____

_____

_____

3) What supernatural event took place during this royal banquet? What did it mean?

_____

_____

_____

_____

_____

_____

4) How did Daniel become involved in this situation? What was his reputation?

_____

_____

_____

_____

_____

_____

# Cross Reference

Read the following passage from Ezekiel 28.

¹ *The word of the LORD came to me again, saying,*

² *"Son of man, say to the prince of Tyre, 'Thus says the Lord GOD: "Because your heart is lifted up, And you say, 'I am a god, I sit in the seat of gods, In the midst of the seas,' Yet you are a man, and not a god, Though you set your heart as the heart of a god*

³ *(Behold, you are wiser than Daniel! There is no secret that can be hidden from you!*

⁴ *With your wisdom and your understanding You have gained riches for yourself, And gathered gold and silver into your treasuries;*

⁵ *By your great wisdom in trade you have increased your riches, And your heart is lifted up because of your riches),"*

⁶ *'Therefore thus says the Lord GOD: "Because you have set your heart as the heart of a god,*

⁷ *Behold, therefore, I will bring strangers against you, The most terrible of the nations; And they shall draw their swords against the beauty of your wisdom, And defile your splendor.*

⁸ *They shall throw you down into the Pit, And you shall die the death of the slain In the midst of the seas.*

⁹ *"Will you still say before him who slays you, 'I am a god'? But you shall be a man, and not a god, In the hand of him who slays you.*

¹⁰ *You shall die the death of the uncircumcised By the hand of aliens; For I have spoken," says the Lord GOD.'"*

# Exploring the Meaning

5) Many Bible scholars believe that this passage in Ezekiel has a dual meaning; that is, it refers not only to a human king but also to Satan. Without getting into that discussion, what does it say about the king of Tyre? In what ways were he and Belshazzar alike? What was their root problem?

_____

_____

_____

6) What was the content of Daniel's interpretation and challenge to Belshazzar? What was his tone as he talked with this Babylonian ruler? Does verse 29 surprise you? Why or why not?

_____

_____

_____

_____

_____

_____

## Summing Up . . .

"Meekness is necessary because we cannot witness effectively without it. Peter says, 'But sanctify the Lord God in your hearts, and always be ready to give a defense to everyone who asks you a reason for the hope that is in you, with meekness and fear' (1 Peter 3:15). Pride will always stand between our testimony and those to whom we testify. They will see us instead of our Lord, no matter how orthodox our theology or how refined our technique."
— John MacArthur

## Reflecting on the Text

7) Daniel had a very good reputation, even among the pagans. How does one develop such respect among unbelievers?

_____

_____

_____

_____

8) How effective are you at speaking hard words of truth to others? Are you too blunt and harsh? Are you too reluctant to make waves? Is loving con-

frontation a natural ability, a supernatural gift, or a skill that can be developed? Why?

_____

_____

_____

_____

_____

9) Ask the Spirit of God to search your heart and reveal any areas in which you are failing to treat God as Holy and as Lord. Write those insights here and then pray for the grace and mercy to live as you should.

_____

_____

_____

_____

_____

_____

## *Recording Your Thoughts*

_____

_____

_____

_____

_____

_____

_____

_____

_____

_____

_____

_____

_____

_____

_____

_____

_____

_____

_____

_____

_____

_____

_____

_____

_____

_____

## *For further study, see the following passages:*

| | | |
|---|---|---|
| 1 Samuel 2:3 | Psalm 62:9 | Isaiah 13 |
| Isaiah 14:12–21 | Isaiah 47 | Jeremiah 50 |
| Jeremiah 51 | Habakkuk 2:5–19 | |

# Daniel in the Lion's Den

Daniel 6:1–28

## *Opening Thought*

1) Who is the most respected Christian in your town or your church? Why? What qualities does this person possess that others admire? How did he or she acquire such a reputation?

_____

_____

_____

_____

_____

2) Suppose that a group of non-Christian neighbors or colleagues from work were sitting around a restaurant table chatting, and your name is suddenly tossed into the conversation. What kind of remarks or comments do you think might be made about you, your character, your lifestyle, and so forth? In other words, what is your reputation in the minds of those who live near you or work with you? Why?

_____

_____

_____

_____

_____

_____

# Background of the Passage

After being transported from Judah to Babylon as a young man, Daniel spent his entire adult life serving as a high-ranking official for pagan kings. This humble, prayerful, and faithful man was God's spokesman to world leaders from approximately 605 to 530 B.C.

Beginning with Babylonian kings Nebuchadnezzar and Belshazzar, Daniel served with distinction. This loyalty continued into the Medo-Persian dynasty under Darius.

Although Daniel's career was not without its difficult and dangerous times, he was a favorite of those whom he served. Daniel possessed experience, wisdom, a sense of history, leadership ability, a sterling reputation, remarkable people skills, a positive attitude, and the benefit of revelation from the God of heaven.

It is not surprising that Daniel's excellence and godliness aroused the ire of the godless men and women around him. The story of Daniel (chapter 6) in the den of lions is a classic example of the evil intent of humans and the sovereign purposes of God.

In short, Daniel demonstrated the evangelistic potential of a godly, uncompromising life. God received great glory from the life and work of this quiet servant.

# Bible Passage

Read 6:1–28, noting the key words and definitions to the right of the passage.

**Daniel 6:1–28**

¹ *It pleased Darius to set over the kingdom one hundred and twenty satraps, to be over the whole kingdom;*

² *and over these, three governors, of whom Daniel was one, that the satraps might give account to them, so that the king would suffer no loss.*

**satraps** (v. 1)—Each is a provincial administrator under the king; Daniel's imminent appointment was to a post as "governor," assisting the king as his vicegerent.

**suffer no loss** (v. 2)—They were responsible to prevent loss from military revolts, tax evasion, and fraud.

³ Then this Daniel distinguished himself above the governors and satraps, because an excellent spirit was in him; and the king gave thought to setting him over the whole realm.

⁴ So the governors and satraps sought to find some charge against Daniel concerning the kingdom; but they could find no charge or fault, because he was faithful; nor was there any error or fault found in him.

⁵ Then these men said, "We shall not find any charge against this Daniel unless we find it against him concerning the law of his God."

⁶ So these governors and satraps thronged before the king, and said thus to him: "King Darius, live forever!

⁷ "All the governors of the kingdom, the administrators and satraps, the counselors and advisors, have consulted together to establish a royal statute and to make a firm decree, that whoever petitions any god or man for thirty days, except you, O king, shall be cast into the den of lions.

⁸ "Now, O king, establish the decree and sign the writing, so that it cannot be changed, according to the law of the Medes and Persians, which does not alter."

⁹ Therefore King Darius signed the written decree.

¹⁰ Now when Daniel knew that the writing was signed, he went home. And in his upper room, with his windows open toward Jerusalem, he knelt down on his knees three times that day, and prayed and gave thanks before his God, as was his custom since early days.

¹¹ Then these men assembled and found Daniel praying and making supplication before his God.

¹² And they went before the king, and spoke concerning the king's decree: "Have you not signed a decree that every man who petitions any god or man within thirty days, except you, O king, shall be cast into the den of lions?" The king answered

**an excellent spirit** (v. 3)—Daniel, over eighty by this time, had enjoyed God's blessings throughout his life.

**over the whole realm** (v. 3)—Apparently God wanted Daniel in this place of influence to encourage and assist in the Jews' return to Judah, since the return was made in Cyrus's first year (539–537 B.C.), right before the lions' den incident.

**charge against Daniel** (v. 4)—a jealous plot, similar to the effort against Daniel's three friends in 3:8.

**King Darius, live forever!** (v. 6)—Ancient kings were frequently worshiped as gods; pagans had such inferior views of their gods that such homage was no problem.

**except you, O king** (v. 7)—A deceptive stroke of the king's ego secured his injunction which was designed to benefit Daniel's peers in the government.

**law . . . which does not alter** (v. 8)—Once enacted, Medo-Persian law could not be changed, even by the king.

**toward Jerusalem** (v. 10)—toward the temple in Jerusalem

**as was his custom** (v. 10)—Daniel was uncompromising in his commitment to seek the Lord.

and said, "The thing is true, according to the law of the Medes and Persians, which does not alter."

13 So they answered and said before the king, "That Daniel, who is one of the captives from Judah, does not show due regard for you, O king, or for the decree that you have signed, but makes his petition three times a day."

14 And the king, when he heard these words, was greatly displeased with himself, and set his heart on Daniel to deliver him; and he labored till the going down of the sun to deliver him.

15 Then these men approached the king, and said to the king, "Know, O king, that it is the law of the Medes and Persians that no decree or statute which the king establishes may be changed."

16 So the king gave the command, and they brought Daniel and cast him into the den of lions. But the king spoke, saying to Daniel, "Your God, whom you serve continually, He will deliver you."

17 Then a stone was brought and laid on the mouth of the den, and the king sealed it with his own signet ring and with the signets of his lords, that the purpose concerning Daniel might not be changed.

18 Now the king went to his palace and spent the night fasting; and no musicians were brought before him. Also his sleep went from him.

19 Then the king arose very early in the morning and went in haste to the den of lions.

20 And when he came to the den, he cried out with a lamenting voice to Daniel. The king spoke, saying to Daniel, "Daniel, servant of the living God, has your God, whom you serve continually, been able to deliver you from the lions?"

21 Then Daniel said to the king, "O king, live forever!

22 "My God sent His angel and shut the lions' mouths, so that they have not hurt me, because I was found innocent before Him; and also, O king, I have done no wrong before you."

**one of the captives from Judah** (v. 13)—Daniel had lived over sixty years in Babylon as a faithful subject; in spite of his loyalty, his faithfulness to God brought this threat.

**displeased with himself** (v. 14)—Darius went from a "god" to a fool in a matter of moments.

**den of lions** (v. 16)—The word suggests an underground pit that probably had a hole at the top from which to drop food and a ramp or hillside with a door through which the lions could enter.

**His angel** (v. 22)—possibly the same person as the fourth person visible in the fiery furnace (see 3:25)

**innocent before Him** (v. 22)—the supreme commendation of Daniel as blameless before God and unworthy of such punishment

23 Then the king was exceedingly glad for him, and commanded that they should take Daniel up out of the den. So Daniel was taken up out of the den, and no injury whatever was found on him, because he believed in his God.

24 And the king gave the command, and they brought those men who had accused Daniel, and they cast them into the den of lions—them, their children, and their wives; and the lions overpowered them, and broke all their bones in pieces before they ever came to the bottom of the den.

25 Then King Darius wrote: To all peoples, nations, and languages that dwell in all the earth: Peace be multiplied to you.

26 I make a decree that in every dominion of my kingdom men must tremble and fear before the God of Daniel. For He is the living God, And steadfast forever; His kingdom is the one which shall not be destroyed, And His dominion shall endure to the end.

27 He delivers and rescues, And He works signs and wonders In heaven and on earth, Who has delivered Daniel from the power of the lions.

28 So this Daniel prospered in the reign of Darius and in the reign of Cyrus the Persian.

**no injury . . . on him** (v. 23)—God openly honored Daniel's faith for the purpose of showing His glory; this is not always the case—God may choose to be glorified in the martyrdom of His saints.

**the king gave the command** (v. 24)—As in the case of Achan (see Joshua 7), this sin against God, Darius, and Daniel cost the men and their families their lives; it also demonstrates the lions were not tame, toothless, or without appetite.

**King Darius wrote** (v. 25)—Impacted by Daniel and the Lord, Darius expressed himself as if he had come to a point of personal trust in God for his salvation.

# Understanding the Text

3) What was the plot against Daniel? What precipitated it?

_____

_____

_____

_____

_____

4) How did Daniel respond to this attempt by enemies to trap and destroy him?

_____

_____

_____

_____

_____

5) How was Daniel vindicated? How did God receive glory?

_____

_____

_____

_____

_____

_____

# Cross Reference

Read the following verses from Genesis 37.

³ *Now Israel loved Joseph more than all his children, because he was the son of his old age. Also he made him a tunic of many colors.*
⁴ *But when his brothers saw that their father loved him more than all his brothers, they hated him and could not speak peaceably to him.*
⁵ *Now Joseph had a dream, and he told it to his brothers; and they hated him even more. . . .*

¹⁸ *Now when they the brothers of Joseph saw him Joseph afar off, even before he came near them, they conspired against him to kill him.*

<sup>19</sup> *Then they said to one another, "Look, this dreamer is coming!*

<sup>20</sup> *"Come therefore, let us now kill him and cast him into some pit; and we shall say, 'Some wild beast has devoured him.' We shall see what will become of his dreams!"*

<sup>21</sup> *But Reuben heard it, and he delivered him out of their hands, and said, "Let us not kill him."*

<sup>22</sup> *And Reuben said to them, "Shed no blood, but cast him into this pit which is in the wilderness, and do not lay a hand on him" —that he might deliver him out of their hands, and bring him back to his father.*

<sup>23</sup> *So it came to pass, when Joseph had come to his brothers, that they stripped Joseph of his tunic, the tunic of many colors that was on him.*

<sup>24</sup> *Then they took him and cast him into a pit. And the pit was empty; there was no water in it.*

<sup>25</sup> *And they sat down to eat a meal. Then they lifted their eyes and looked, and there was a company of Ishmaelites, coming from Gilead with their camels, bearing spices, balm, and myrrh, on their way to carry them down to Egypt.*

<sup>26</sup> *So Judah said to his brothers, "What profit is there if we kill our brother and conceal his blood?*

<sup>27</sup> *"Come and let us sell him to the Ishmaelites, and let not our hand be upon him, for he is our brother and our flesh." And his brothers listened.*

<sup>28</sup> *Then Midianite traders passed by; so the brothers pulled Joseph up and lifted him out of the pit, and sold him to the Ishmaelites for twenty shekels of silver. And they took Joseph to Egypt.*

# *Exploring the Meaning*

6) Just as Daniel's colleagues were jealous of his success, the brothers of Joseph were jealous of his favoritism. What do these episodes demonstrate about the power of unchecked jealousy? What prompts such deep emotion?

_____

_____

_____

_____

_____

_____

7) Read Genesis 45:3–8. The story of Joseph is a powerful example of God's sovereignty. How do you see the sovereign hand of God in chapter 6?

_____

_____

_____

_____

_____

8) Why was King Darius so upset about being forced (by the law he enacted) to throw Daniel to the lions? What are the implications of the last half of 6:17?

_____

_____

_____

_____

_____

_____

## Summing Up . . .

"It is especially easy for Christians who live in a free and prosperous society to feel secure just as they are, presuming on instead of depending on God's grace. It is easy to become so satisfied with physical blessings that we have little desire for spiritual blessings, and to become so dependent on our physical resources that we feel little need for spiritual resources. When programs, methods, and money produce such obvious and impressive results, there is a proneness to confuse human success with divine blessing. A happy marriage, well-behaved children, and a church that is growing tend to make people smug and self-satisfied. They can even become practical humanists, living as though God were not necessary. When that happens, passionate longing for God and yearning for His help will be missing—along with God's empowerment."— _John MacArthur_

# *Reflecting on the Text*

9) What strikes you about Daniel's habit of prayer? Why do you think he was so committed to this discipline? How much do you depend on God and yearn for His presence and power? What needs to change?

_____

_____

_____

_____

10) Daniel was spared and delivered; other saints (for example, John the Baptist—Matthew 14:10–11; Stephen—Acts 7:59) were not. Why? How does God get glory from the martyrdom of His children?

_____

_____

_____

_____

_____

11) When Daniel's enemies went digging through his personal life in their attempt to accuse him of something illegal, the worst they discovered about him was that he was a man of prayer! If someone were to secretly bug your house and follow you everywhere, what would that person learn about you? Would he or she find evidence that would undermine your credibility? What specifically needs to change in your life today?

_____

_____

_____

_____

## Recording Your Thoughts

_____

_____

_____

_____

_____

_____

_____

_____

_____

_____

_____

_____

_____

_____

_____

_____

_____

### For further study, see the following passages:

| | | |
|---|---|---|
| Joshua 7:20–26 | 1 Kings 8:44–45 | Esther 1:19 |
| Esther 8:8 | Psalm 55:16–17 | Proverbs 21:1 |
| Daniel 5:13 | Matthew 5:48 | Hebrews 11:33–38 |

# Daniel's Visions

## Opening Thought

1) The arrival of a new millennium sparked unusual interest in spiritual matters and in questions about the future. What strange ideas, beliefs, and practices have you observed as people discuss the future?

_____

_____

_____

_____

_____

_____

_____

_____

_____

_____

_____

_____

_____

_____

_____

_____

# Background of the Passage

Chapter 7, like chapter 2, reveals the prophetic course of Gentile dominion on the earth. This time, God revealed His purposes directly to His servant, Daniel, rather than through a pagan king. Also the symbolism in Daniel's dream differs from the imagery in Nebuchadnezzar's dream (chapter 2). Whereas Nebuchadnezzar saw a giant image or statue, with various parts that represented a series of world empires, Daniel saw a collection of beasts and creatures. The prophet's dream moved far beyond his own day to the coming of Israel's Messiah/King to end all Gentile kingdoms and to establish His eternal kingdom.

This chapter (as well as the whole book) is significant for a number of reasons: (1) it demonstrates God's sovereignty over earthly affairs and human history; (2) it provides a clear glimpse of the prophetic future—specifically the events leading up to the Second Advent of Christ; (3) it shows the veracity of the Word of God (in the numerous prophecies already fulfilled in history); (4) it gives believers a wonderful role model in the person of Daniel, who lived a life of faithfulness and devotion.

Ask God to open your eyes to the profound truths and lessons of chapter 7.

# Bible Passage

Read 7:1–28, noting the key words and definitions to the right of the passage.

## Daniel 7:1–28

¹ In the first year of Belshazzar king of Babylon, Daniel had a dream and visions of his head while on his bed. Then he wrote down the dream, telling the main facts.
² Daniel spoke, saying, "I saw in my vision by night, and behold, the four winds of heaven were stirring up the Great Sea.
³ "And four great beasts came up from the sea, each different from the other.
⁴ "The first was like a lion, and had eagle's wings. I watched till its wings were plucked off; and it

**first year** (v. 1)—a flashback to 553 B.C., fourteen years before the feast of 5:1–3; chapters 7 and 8 occur after chapter 4 but before chapter 5

**Great Sea** (v. 2)—a reference to the Mediterranean; symbolic of the nations and peoples

**four . . . beasts** (v. 3)—representing the same kingdoms as the image in chapter 2

**lion . . . wings** (v. 4)—The vicious, powerful, swift king of

was lifted up from the earth and made to stand on two feet like a man, and a man's heart was given to it.

5 "And suddenly another beast, a second, like a bear. It was raised up on one side, and had three ribs in its mouth between its teeth. And they said thus to it: 'Arise, devour much flesh!'

6 "After this I looked, and there was another, like a leopard, which had on its back four wings of a bird. The beast also had four heads, and dominion was given to it.

7 "After this I saw in the night visions, and behold, a fourth beast, dreadful and terrible, exceedingly strong. It had huge iron teeth; it was devouring, breaking in pieces, and trampling the residue with its feet. It was different from all the beasts that were before it, and it had ten horns.

8 "I was considering the horns, and there was another horn, a little one, coming up among them, before whom three of the first horns were plucked out by the roots. And there, in this horn, were eyes like the eyes of a man, and a mouth speaking pompous words.

9 "I watched till thrones were put in place, And the Ancient of Days was seated; His garment was white as snow, And the hair of His head was like pure wool. His throne was a fiery flame, Its wheels a burning fire;

10 A fiery stream issued And came forth from before Him. A thousand thousands ministered to Him; Ten thousand times ten thousand stood before Him. The court was seated, And the books were opened.

11 "I watched then because of the sound of the pompous words which the horn was speaking; I watched till the beast was slain, and its body destroyed and given to the burning flame.

12 "As for the rest of the beasts, they had their dominion taken away, yet their lives were prolonged for a season and a time.

beasts represents Babylon in this vision. Lions guarded the gates of the royal palaces of Babylon.

**a bear** (v. 5)—This is Medo-Persia, with the greater "side" being Persia and the "ribs" referring to vanquished nations.

**a leopard** (v. 6)—This is Greece, with its fleetness in conquest under Alexander the Great (born in 356 B.C.).

**four heads** (v. 6)—This represents the four generals who divided the kingdom after Alexander's death at age thirty-three (323 B.C.).

**fourth beast** (v. 7)—No such animal exists; rather this creature points to the Roman Empire, devastating in conquest. Roman dominion fell apart in A.D. 476, yet it lived on in divided status (Europe) and will be revived and returned to strength near Christ's second coming.

**ten horns** (v. 7)—ten kings

**another horn** (v. 8)—This speaks of the rise of Antichrist, a real human filled with pride.

**I watched** (v. 9)—The vision flashed forward to the divine throne from which judgment will come upon the fourth kingdom.

**the beast was slain** (v. 11)—The fourth beast, headed by Antichrist, will be destroyed at the second coming of Christ.

**rest of the beasts** (v. 12)—the three earlier beasts (empires of chapters 2 and 7) that lost their dominance when conquered, though each was amalgamated into the victorious empire and survived in its descendancy.

13 *"I was watching in the night visions, And behold, One like the Son of Man, Coming with the clouds of heaven! He came to the Ancient of Days, And they brought Him near before Him.*

14 *Then to Him was given dominion and glory and a kingdom, That all peoples, nations, and languages should serve Him. His dominion is an everlasting dominion, Which shall not pass away, And His kingdom the one Which shall not be destroyed.*

15 *"I, Daniel, was grieved in my spirit within my body, and the visions of my head troubled me.*

16 *"I came near to one of those who stood by, and asked him the truth of all this. So he told me and made known to me the interpretation of these things:*

17 *'Those great beasts, which are four, are four kings which arise out of the earth.*

18 *'But the saints of the Most High shall receive the kingdom, and possess the kingdom forever, even forever and ever.'*

19 *"Then I wished to know the truth about the fourth beast, which was different from all the others, exceedingly dreadful, with its teeth of iron and its nails of bronze, which devoured, broke in pieces, and trampled the residue with its feet;*

20 *"and the ten horns that were on its head, and the other horn which came up, before which three fell, namely, that horn which had eyes and a mouth which spoke pompous words, whose appearance was greater than his fellows.*

21 *"I was watching; and the same horn was making war against the saints, and prevailing against them,*

22 *"until the Ancient of Days came, and a judgment was made in favor of the saints of the Most High, and the time came for the saints to possess the kingdom.*

23 *"Thus he said: 'The fourth beast shall be A fourth kingdom on earth, Which shall be differ-*

**Son of Man** (v. 13)—the Messiah, distinct from the Ancient of Days or Eternal One, the Father

**all peoples, nations, and languages** (v. 14)—These earthly distinctions speak of the promise of an earthly kingdom ruled by Christ that will merge into an eternal kingdom.

**grieved in my spirit** (v. 15)—The prospect of coming judgment made Daniel sad.

**those who stood by** (v. 16)—Angels helped Daniel understand God's revelation.

**beasts . . . four** (v. 17)—Babylon, Medo-Persia, Greece, and Rome

**saints** (v. 18)—Those who had trusted God possessed the kingdom headed up by the Son of Man, the Messiah.

**the Most High** (v. 18)—God is referred to in this book as being above all gods.

**fourth beast . . . different** (v. 19)—a possible reference to greater diversity or greater breadth of conquest; it will branch out into two great divisions (that is, "legs"), then near the end into ten horns (a confederacy of ten nations)

**the other horn** (v. 20)—An eleventh horn (Antichrist's kingdom) will arise before Christ's second coming.

**war against the saints** (v. 21)—a great persecution against believers led by Antichrist, especially in Israel

**Ancient of Days** (v. 22)—a reference to God the Father, the Eternal One

ent *from all other kingdoms, And shall devour the whole earth, Trample it and break it in pieces.*

24 *The ten horns are ten kings Who shall arise from this kingdom. And another shall rise after them; He shall be different from the first ones, And shall subdue three kings.*

25 *He shall speak pompous words against the Most High, Shall persecute the saints of the Most High, And shall intend to change times and law. Then the saints shall be given into his hand For a time and times and half a time.*

26 *'But the court shall be seated, And they shall take away his dominion, To consume and destroy it forever.*

27 *Then the kingdom and dominion, And the greatness of the kingdoms under the whole heaven, Shall be given to the people, the saints of the Most High. His kingdom is an everlasting kingdom, And all dominions shall serve and obey Him.'*

28 *"This is the end of the account. As for me, Daniel, my thoughts greatly troubled me, and my countenance changed; but I kept the matter in my heart."*

**judgment** (v. 22)—against Antichrist and the unsaved

**saints to possess the kingdom** (v. 22)—Believers will enter the kingdom in its earthly, millennial phase following Christ's second coming. They will have eternal life that will continue into the eternal state after the thousand years.

**another . . . after them** (v. 24)—This "little horn" (Antichrist) blasts his way to the zenith of world rule.

**time and times and half a time** (v. 25)—an obvious reference to the three and a half years which are the last half of the seven-year period of Antichrist's power

**the court** (v. 26)—God will have His court session to judge sinners and sin; He will remove the Antichrist's rule and destroy him and his empire in eternal, conscious hell.

**the kingdom . . . given to . . . the saints** (v. 27)—God's kingdom in both earthly and heavenly phases

# *Understanding the Text*

2) What four beasts did Daniel see in his vision and what did they represent? In what ways was the fourth beast different from the others?

_____

_____

_____

_____

_____

3) Describe the pertinent details surrounding Daniel's vision of the "Ancient of Days." How is God portrayed in this passage?

_____

_____

_____

_____

_____

4) How did Daniel discover the meaning of these visions? Were the visions more comforting or more troubling? Why?

_____

_____

_____

_____

_____

# Cross Reference

Consider this passage from Revelation 13.

¹ *Then I stood on the sand of the sea. And I saw a beast rising up out of the sea, having seven heads and ten horns, and on his horns ten crowns, and on his heads a blasphemous name.*

² *Now the beast which I saw was like a leopard, his feet were like the feet of a bear, and his mouth like the mouth of a lion. The dragon gave him his power, his throne, and great authority.*

³ *And I saw one of his heads as if it had been mortally wounded, and his deadly wound was healed. And all the world marveled and followed the beast.*

⁴ *So they worshiped the dragon who gave authority to the beast; and they worshiped the beast, saying, "Who is like the beast? Who is able to make war with him?"*

⁵ *And he was given a mouth speaking great things and blasphemies, and he was given authority to continue for forty-two months.*

⁶ *Then he opened his mouth in blasphemy against God, to blaspheme His name, His tabernacle, and those who dwell in heaven.*

⁷ *It was granted to him to make war with the saints and to overcome them. And authority was given him over every tribe, tongue, and nation.*

⁸ *All who dwell on the earth will worship him, whose names have not been written in the Book of Life of the Lamb slain from the foundation of the world.*

⁹ *If anyone has an ear, let him hear.*

¹⁰ *He who leads into captivity shall go into captivity; he who kills with the sword must be killed with the sword. Here is the patience and the faith of the saints.*

¹¹ *Then I saw another beast coming up out of the earth, and he had two horns like a lamb and spoke like a dragon.*

¹² *And he exercises all the authority of the first beast in his presence, and causes the earth and those who dwell in it to worship the first beast, whose deadly wound was healed.*

¹³ *He performs great signs, so that he even makes fire come down from heaven on the earth in the sight of men.*

¹⁴ *And he deceives those who dwell on the earth by those signs which he was granted to do in the sight of the beast, telling those who dwell on the earth to make an image to the beast who was wounded by the sword and lived.*

¹⁵ *He was granted power to give breath to the image of the beast, that the image of the beast should both speak and cause as many as would not worship the image of the beast to be killed.*

¹⁶ *He causes all, both small and great, rich and poor, free and slave, to receive a mark on their right hand or on their foreheads,*

¹⁷ *and that no one may buy or sell except one who has the mark or the name of the beast, or the number of his name.*

¹⁸ *Here is wisdom. Let him who has understanding calculate the number of the beast, for it is the number of a man: His number is six hundred and sixty-six.*

## *Exploring the Meaning*

5) What does John's vision add to the revelation from Daniel's vision that the "same horn was making war against the saints" (verse 21)?

_____

_____

_____

6) In his description of Antichrist (the leader of Daniel's fourth beast or empire), Revelation uses the imagery of a leopard, bear, and lion (which is how Daniel described his first three beasts)? Why do you think this is so?

_____

_____

_____

_____

_____

7) Re-read Daniel 2:20–22. What truths does this prayer of praise contain for those who might be tempted to worry about the future?

_____

_____

_____

_____

_____

_____

## Summing Up . . .

"Perhaps no subject in Scripture is more intriguing than the second coming of Jesus Christ, and none should be more motivating to the believer and unbeliever alike. 'Knowing, therefore, the terror of the Lord,' Paul declared, 'we persuade men' (2 Corinthians 5:11). Realizing that Christ will one day come in terrible judgment, the sensible believer should be motivated to faithfully present the gospel to unbelievers in order that they might have the opportunity to be saved. The faithful Christian is also motivated by the reward he will receive when His Lord returns, and with Paul he has the 'aim, whether present or absent, to be well pleasing to Him' (2 Cor.5:9)."
—John MacArthur

# *Reflecting on the Text*

8) What people in your life seem to be most interested in spiritual matters? How can you use fascination with the end times to witness to unbelieving neighbors, friends, family members, and colleagues?

_____

_____

_____

_____

_____

9) Daniel's vision of God says that "the hair of His head was like pure wool." What should we gather from this, and what conclusions should we not make? What Daniel saw defied human words and explanations; yet, he sought to put it into words nonetheless, knowing that the words could never fully do justice to what he had seen. Thus the descriptions given should not be taken as literal. Why is it dangerous to speak of what God looks like? How would you describe God for a small child?

_____

_____

_____

_____

10) Daniel mentioned his grief over the vision of coming judgment. On a scale of 1–10 (with 1 being "not at all" and 10 being "deeply, terribly!") how troubled are you by the direction of your culture? What do you plan (specifically) to do about it this week?

_____

_____

_____

_____

# *Recording Your Thoughts*

_____

_____

_____

_____

_____

_____

_____

_____

_____

_____

_____

_____

_____

_____

_____

_____

_____

_____

_____

_____

_____

## *For further study, see the following passages:*

| | | |
|---|---|---|
| Genesis 14:19–22 | 2 Kings 5:17 | Daniel 2:35, 45 |
| Matthew 24:15–22 | 2 Thessalonians 2:3–10 | Revelation 12:13–17 |
| Revelation 13:1–10 | Revelation 20:1–4, 11–15 | Revelation 21:27 |
| Revelation 22:3–4, 14 | | |

# Prophecy of the Ram and the Male Goat

Daniel 8:1–27

## Opening Thought

1) What kind of a history student were or are you? Do you enjoy learning about past events and long ago civilizations? Why?

_____

_____

_____

_____

_____

_____

2) If you could take a week to visit any culture and any period of human history, what era would you like to investigate? Why?

_____

_____

_____

_____

_____

_____

_____

# Background of the Passage

The Book of Daniel can be divided into three broad sections: (1) the personal background of Daniel the prophet (1:1–21); (2) the prophetic course of Gentile dominion (2:1—7:28); and (3) the prophetic course of Israel's destiny (8:1—12:13). We now turn to this third topic.

Chapter 8 reveals Daniel's vision of a ram and a goat. The ram is a picture of the Medo-Persian Empire, the two horns standing for the two entities (the Medes and the Persians) that merged into one. The goat represents Macedonian Greece with its great horn, Alexander, who with his army of thirty-five thousand men moved with such speed that he is pictured as not even touching the ground. His death (in 323 B.C.), and the division of his world empire among his four generals are prefigured.

The chapter also prophetically outlines the career of Antiochus Epiphanes (175–164 B.C.), called the "little horn," who, in his idolatry and desecration of the temple, would foreshadow the little horn of chapter 7, that is, the Antichrist (see Revelation 13).

Only with the help of the angel Gabriel was Daniel able to interpret this vision. It serves as a great reminder of the faithfulness of God. Not even when God's covenant people are under divine discipline does He forsake them. On the contrary he deals patiently with them and will ultimately bring them to a place of unparalleled blessing.

# Bible Passage

Read 8:1–27, noting the key words and definitions to the right of the passage.

## Daniel 8:1–27

¹ *In the third year of the reign of King Belshazzar a vision appeared to me—to me, Daniel—after the one that appeared to me the first time.*
² *I saw in the vision, and it so happened while I was looking, that I was in Shushan, the citadel, which is in the province of Elam; and I saw in the vision that I was by the River Ulai.*

**third year** (v. 1)—551 B.C., two years after the dream of chapter 7 but before chapter 5

**the first time** (v. 1)—looks back to chapter 7

**Shushan** (v. 2)—Called Susa by the Greeks, this was a chief city of the Medo-Persian Empire and was located about 250 miles east of Babylon.

³ Then I lifted my eyes and saw, and there, standing beside the river, was a ram which had two horns, and the two horns were high; but one was higher than the other, and the higher one came up last.

⁴ I saw the ram pushing westward, northward, and southward, so that no animal could withstand him; nor was there any that could deliver from his hand, but he did according to his will and became great.

⁵ And as I was considering, suddenly a male goat came from the west, across the surface of the whole earth, without touching the ground; and the goat had a notable horn between his eyes.

⁶ Then he came to the ram that had two horns, which I had seen standing beside the river, and ran at him with furious power.

⁷ And I saw him confronting the ram; he was moved with rage against him, attacked the ram, and broke his two horns. There was no power in the ram to withstand him, but he cast him down to the ground and trampled him; and there was no one that could deliver the ram from his hand.

⁸ Therefore the male goat grew very great; but when he became strong, the large horn was broken, and in place of it four notable ones came up toward the four winds of heaven.

⁹ And out of one of them came a little horn which grew exceedingly great toward the south, toward the east, and toward the Glorious Land.

¹⁰ And it grew up to the host of heaven; and it cast down some of the host and some of the stars to the ground, and trampled them.

¹¹ He even exalted himself as high as the Prince of the host; and by him the daily sacrifices were taken away, and the place of His sanctuary was cast down.

¹² Because of transgression, an army was given over to the horn to oppose the daily sacrifices; and he

**ram** (v. 3)—the Medo-Persian Empire

**no animal could withstand him** (v. 4)—a reference to the conquests under Cyrus (as predicted by Isaiah some 150 years earlier)

**goat** (v. 5)—Greece, led by Alexander the Great

**large horn was broken** (v. 8)—the death of Alexander the Great

**four notable ones** (v. 8)—the four generals who became kings over four sectors of the Grecian empire following Alexander's death

**Glorious Land** (v. 9)—Palestine

**host of heaven** (v. 10)—picturesque language using the figure of stars to portray Antiochus's persecution of Jews

**Prince** (v. 11)—Antiochus not only desecrated the temple, but he also blasphemed Christ to whom the sanctuary belongs and to whom the sacrifices point.

**holy one** (v. 12)—Angels are in view here.

**two thousand three hundred days** (v. 14)—2,300 total days, or about six and a half years of sacrificing a lamb twice a day; this prophecy precisely identified the time as that of Antiochus's persecution, September 6, 171 B.C. to December 25, 165/4 B.C.; after his death the Jews celebrated the cleansing of their holy place, led by Judas Maccabeus, in the Feast of Lights or Hanukkah

**appearance of a man** (v. 15)—The word means "a mighty man" and is the linguistic framework for

*cast truth down to the ground. He did all this and prospered.*

13 *Then I heard a holy one speaking; and another holy one said to that certain one who was speaking, "How long will the vision be, concerning the daily sacrifices and the transgression of desolation, the giving of both the sanctuary and the host to be trampled under foot?"*

14 *And he said to me, "For two thousand three hundred days; then the sanctuary shall be cleansed."*

15 *Then it happened, when I, Daniel, had seen the vision and was seeking the meaning, that suddenly there stood before me one having the appearance of a man.*

16 *And I heard a man's voice between the banks of the Ulai, who called, and said, "Gabriel, make this man understand the vision."*

17 *So he came near where I stood, and when he came I was afraid and fell on my face; but he said to me, "Understand, son of man, that the vision refers to the time of the end."*

18 *Now, as he was speaking with me, I was in a deep sleep with my face to the ground; but he touched me, and stood me upright.*

19 *And he said, "Look, I am making known to you what shall happen in the latter time of the indignation; for at the appointed time the end shall be.*

20 *"The ram which you saw, having the two horns—they are the kings of Media and Persia.*

21 *"And the male goat is the kingdom of Greece. The large horn that is between its eyes is the first king.*

22 *"As for the broken horn and the four that stood up in its place, four kingdoms shall arise out of that nation, but not with its power.*

23 *"And in the latter time of their kingdom, When the transgressors have reached their fullness, A king shall arise, Having fierce features, Who understands sinister schemes.*

24 *His power shall be mighty, but not by his own*

"Gabriel"; this is the first time an angel is named in Scripture.

**a man's voice** (v. 16)—God spoke with a human voice.

**afraid and fell** (v. 17)—Loss of consciousness is a common reaction to heavenly visitation.

**time of the end** (v. 17)—The term likely has a dual meaning, referring to a time late in the period defined by the empires described in these verses and also to the last days of human history at the time of Antichrist.

**male goat . . . large horn** (v. 21)—Greece, the third Gentile world power, led by Alexander the Great

**broken horn and . . . four** (v. 22)—Alexander died at age thirty-three, leaving no heir ready to reign, so the empire (after a twenty-two-year battle for control) was placed under the control of four generals: Cassander (Macedonia); Lysimachus (Thrace and Asia Minor); Seleucus (Syria and Babylonia); and Ptolemy (Egypt and Arabia).

**A king shall arise** (v. 23)—The near fulfillment is seen in Antiochus; the far fulfillment will take place when Antichrist rises to power in the final tribulation period.

**seal up the vision** (v. 26)—not a command for secrecy but for preservation as truth even though the fulfillment was not for a long time

power; He shall destroy fearfully, And shall prosper and thrive; He shall destroy the mighty, and
also the holy people.

25 "Through his cunning He shall cause deceit to
prosper under his rule; And he shall exalt himself
in his heart. He shall destroy many in their prosperity. He shall even rise against the Prince of
princes; But he shall be broken without human
means.

26 "And the vision of the evenings and mornings
Which was told is true; Therefore seal up the
vision, For it refers to many days in the future."

27 And I, Daniel, fainted and was sick for days;
afterward I arose and went about the king's business. I was astonished by the vision, but no one
understood it.

# Understanding the Text

3) What kinds of creatures did Daniel see in his vision and what were they
doing?

_____

_____

_____

_____

_____

4) Who helped Daniel understand the meaning of the vision?

_____

_____

_____

_____

5) How does history confirm the statements and descriptions found in chapter 8?

_____

_____

_____

_____

_____

_____

# Cross Reference

Read the following passage from 2 Thessalonians 2.

¹ *Now, brethren, concerning the coming of our Lord Jesus Christ and our gathering together to Him, we ask you,*

² *not to be soon shaken in mind or troubled, either by spirit or by word or by letter, as if from us, as though the day of Christ had come.*

³ *Let no one deceive you by any means; for that Day will not come unless the falling away comes first, and the man of sin is revealed, the son of perdition,*

⁴ *who opposes and exalts himself above all that is called God or that is worshiped, so that he sits as God in the temple of God, showing himself that he is God.*

⁵ *Do you not remember that when I was still with you I told you these things?*

⁶ *And now you know what is restraining, that he may be revealed in his own time.*

⁷ *For the mystery of lawlessness is already at work; only He who now restrains will do so until He is taken out of the way.*

⁸ *And then the lawless one will be revealed, whom the Lord will consume with the breath of His mouth and destroy with the brightness of His coming.*

⁹ *The coming of the lawless one is according to the working of Satan, with all power, signs, and lying wonders,*

¹⁰ *and with all unrighteous deception among those who perish, because they did not receive the love of the truth, that they might be saved.*

¹¹ *And for this reason God will send them strong delusion, that they should believe the lie,*

¹² *that they all may be condemned who did not believe the truth but had pleasure in unrighteousness.*

# *Exploring the Meaning*

6) What does Paul say here must occur before the Second Coming of Christ?

_____

_____

_____

_____

_____

_____

7) Why do you think Daniel became afraid and fell when Gabriel came near?

_____

_____

_____

_____

_____

_____

(verses to consider: Luke 1:13, 30; 2:10)

8) Re-read 8:27. How do you account for this effect (of the vision) on Daniel?

_____

_____

_____

_____

_____

_____

# Summing Up . . .

"As Jesus Christ was righteousness incarnate, the Antichrist will be evil incarnate. In the book of Daniel he is called an insolent king, skilled in intrigue (8:23), a self-willed tyrant who magnifies himself above every god and speaks monstrous evil against the God of gods (11:36). Paul calls him the man of lawlessness and the son of destruction (2 Thessalonians 2:3) and in the book of Revelation he is called the beast (11:7; 13:1–10)." —*John MacArthur*

# Reflecting on the Text

9) What is the value of studying prophecy in Scripture? How can it benefit a Christian?

_____

_____

_____

_____

_____

_____

10) In the Bible, angelic visitations are always associated with major acts of God (for example, the destruction of Sodom and Gomorrah, the birth of Christ, the resurrection of Christ; prophecies about the return of Christ). In what ways does this theocentric (that is, God-centered) angelology differ from modern society's beliefs about angels?

_____

_____

_____

_____

_____

_____

11) How could you use this chapter (and its accurate prophecies about Antiochus) to share the truth about the end-times with an unbeliever?

_____

_____

_____

_____

_____

_____

## *Recording Your Thoughts*

_____

_____

_____

_____

_____

_____

_____

_____

_____

_____

_____

_____

_____

_____

_____

*For further study, see the following passages:*

| | | |
|---|---|---|
| Genesis 12:3 | Exodus 12:41 | Deuteronomy 1:10 |
| Isaiah 6 | Isaiah 45:1–7 | Ezekiel 1 |
| Ezekiel 8 | Daniel 11:2–35 | Revelation 1 |

# The Prophecy of the 70 Weeks

## Opening Thought

1) When have you prayed most fervently and intensely for something? What was it? What happened?

_____

_____

_____

_____

2) What's the most startling answer to prayer you've ever received?

_____

_____

_____

_____

_____

3) When have you prayed for something and then later been relieved or even glad God didn't answer that request in the affirmative? What? Why?

_____

_____

_____

_____

_____

# Background of the Passage

Chapter 9 begins with Daniel studying Jeremiah's prophecies concerning Judah's seventy-year exile (Jeremiah 25:11–12; 29:10). With Darius's recent victory over the Babylonians, Daniel may have been motivated to gain a deeper understanding of God's actions and intentions in national and international affairs. As he studied, Daniel recognized that the time of the nation's captivity was drawing to a close. Filled with hope for his people's imminent restoration, he began to fast and pray.

Daniel's prayer stands as a model of genuine, heartfelt intercession. A response to the revealed truth of God, it is characterized by humility, confession, and self-denial with the ultimate goal to glorify God. The focal point of the chapter, however, is the theologically complex and startlingly accurate prophecy regarding the future of Israel that came to Daniel as a response to his prayer via the angel Gabriel.

Using the figure of 70 weeks (weeks of years, or 490 years total), God declared through His angelic messenger: (1) a period of 7 weeks (that is, 49 years—the time it took to finish rebuilding the city of Jerusalem, a project begun by the decree of Artaxerxes in 444 B.C.); (2) a consecutive period of 62 weeks (that is, 434 years—from 395 B.C. until Christ's triumphal entry into Jerusalem in A.D. 30, just before he was "cut off" or crucified); (3) followed by an indeterminate period of national rejection, highlighted by the destruction of Jerusalem in A.D. 70, and a final week (that is, 7 years or Daniel's so-called 70th week), that would constitute the climax of Jewish history prior to the inauguration of Messiah's millennial kingdom.

The details and meaning of this 70th week has been the subject of intense debate over the years. A straightforward reading of the text and comparisons with related passages in the New Testament, however, reveals a clear and breathtaking future for Israel and the world.

Again the amazing prophecies of Daniel demonstrate the Lord's sovereignty and power as well as His faithfulness to His people.

# Bible Passage

Read 9:1–27, noting the key words and definitions to the right of the passage.

## Daniel 9:1–27

1 *In the first year of Darius the son of Ahasuerus, of the lineage of the Medes, who was made king over the realm of the Chaldeans—*

2 *in the first year of his reign I, Daniel, understood by the books the number of the years specified by the word of the LORD through Jeremiah the prophet, that He would accomplish seventy years in the desolations of Jerusalem.*

3 *Then I set my face toward the Lord God to make request by prayer and supplications, with fasting, sackcloth, and ashes.*

4 *And I prayed to the LORD my God, and made confession, and said, "O Lord, great and awesome God, who keeps His covenant and mercy with those who love Him, and with those who keep His commandments,*

5 *"we have sinned and committed iniquity, we have done wickedly and rebelled, even by departing from Your precepts and Your judgments.*

6 *"Neither have we heeded Your servants the prophets, who spoke in Your name to our kings and our princes, to our fathers and all the people of the land.*

7 *"O Lord, righteousness belongs to You, but to us shame of face, as it is this day—to the men of Judah, to the inhabitants of Jerusalem and all Israel, those near and those far off in all the countries to which You have driven them, because of the unfaithfulness which they have committed against You.*

8 *"O Lord, to us belongs shame of face, to our kings, our princes, and our fathers, because we have sinned against You.*

9 *"To the Lord our God belong mercy and forgive-*

**the first year** (v. 1)—539 B.C.

**made king** (v. 1)—This may mean that Darius (a title, not a proper name) refers to Cyrus, who was made king by God's allowance.

**seventy years** (v. 2)—Daniel's study of "the books" (Old Testament scrolls) focused on the years prophesied for the captivity by Jeremiah. Since the end of that span was near, he prayed for God's next move on behalf of Israel.

**fasting, sackcloth, and ashes** (v. 3)—signifying true repentance; fervency and a deep heart-level desire to be clean before God

**I prayed** (v. 4)—Daniel's prayer gives rich insight into the nature and practice of God-honoring prayer.

**we have sinned** (v. 5)—a clear, unambiguous admission of rebellion

**To the Lord our God belong mercy and forgiveness** (v. 9)—Daniel rooted his request in the perfect character of God.

**the curse** (v. 11)—the judgment brought by God on Israel for her disobedience in the Land; in contrast to the blessings associated with faith and obedience

**let Your anger . . . be turned away** (v. 16)—a prayer for restoration in three aspects: God's city, God's sanctuary, and God's people

**the man Gabriel** (v. 21)—This

ness, *though we have rebelled against Him.*

10 *"We have not obeyed the voice of the* LORD *our God, to walk in His laws, which He set before us by His servants the prophets.*

11 *"Yes, all Israel has transgressed Your law, and has departed so as not to obey Your voice; therefore the curse and the oath written in the Law of Moses the servant of God have been poured out on us, because we have sinned against Him.*

12 *"And He has confirmed His words, which He spoke against us and against our judges who judged us, by bringing upon us a great disaster; for under the whole heaven such has never been done as what has been done to Jerusalem.*

13 *"As it is written in the Law of Moses, all this disaster has come upon us; yet we have not made our prayer before the* LORD *our God, that we might turn from our iniquities and understand Your truth.*

14 *"Therefore the* LORD *has kept the disaster in mind, and brought it upon us; for the* LORD *our God is righteous in all the works which He does, though we have not obeyed His voice.*

15 *"And now, O Lord our God, who brought Your people out of the land of Egypt with a mighty hand, and made Yourself a name, as it is this day—we have sinned, we have done wickedly!*

16 *"O Lord, according to all Your righteousness, I pray, let Your anger and Your fury be turned away from Your city Jerusalem, Your holy mountain; because for our sins, and for the iniquities of our fathers, Jerusalem and Your people are a reproach to all those around us.*

17 *"Now therefore, our God, hear the prayer of Your servant, and his supplications, and for the Lord's sake cause Your face to shine on Your sanctuary, which is desolate.*

18 *"O my God, incline Your ear and hear; open Your eyes and see our desolations, and the city which is called by Your name; for we do not present our*

angel is described as a man because he appeared in human form.

***Seventy weeks . . . Until***
(9:24–25)—weeks of years (see 10:2–3 where weeks of days are described in a different way); the time spans from the Persian Artaxerxes's decree to rebuild Jerusalem (445 B.C.) to Messiah's kingdom

***to finish . . . to make . . . to bring*** (v. 24)—with regard to sin God pledged to "finish the transgression" (that is, restrain sin); to "make an end of sins" (that is, to judge it with finality); and to "make reconciliation for iniquity" (that is, atonement for sin through the blood of a Messiah who would be "cut off"); these prophecies were fulfilled in principle at Christ's first coming

***to bring . . . to seal . . . to anoint*** (v. 24)—With regard to righteousness, God promised: to "bring in . . . righteousness" (that is, eternal righteousness after a long history of national apostasy), "seal up vision" (that is, end the need for revelations), and "anoint the Most Holy" (that is, consecrate the Holy Place in a temple of the future that will be the center of worship in the millennial kingdom of Messiah). These will be fulfilled at Christ's Second Advent.

***seven weeks*** (v. 25)—49 years, possibly closing Nehemiah's career in the rebuilding of the "street and wall," as well as the end of the ministry of Malachi and the close of the Old Testament

***sixty-two weeks*** (v. 25)—434 years, for a total of 483 years to the first advent of Messiah; this was fulfilled to the day on 9 Nisan, A.D. 30 when Christ entered Jerusalem on the colt of a donkey

supplications before You because of our righteous deeds, but because of Your great mercies.

19 "O Lord, hear! O Lord, forgive! O Lord, listen and act! Do not delay for Your own sake, my God, for Your city and Your people are called by Your name."

20 Now while I was speaking, praying, and confessing my sin and the sin of my people Israel, and presenting my supplication before the LORD my God for the holy mountain of my God,

21 yes, while I was speaking in prayer, the man Gabriel, whom I had seen in the vision at the beginning, being caused to fly swiftly, reached me about the time of the evening offering.

22 And he informed me, and talked with me, and said, "O Daniel, I have now come forth to give you skill to understand.

23 "At the beginning of your supplications the command went out, and I have come to tell you, for you are greatly beloved; therefore consider the matter, and understand the vision:

24 "Seventy weeks are determined For your people and for your holy city, To finish the transgression, To make an end of sins, To make reconciliation for iniquity, To bring in everlasting righteousness, To seal up vision and prophecy, And to anoint the Most Holy.

25 "Know therefore and understand, That from the going forth of the command To restore and build Jerusalem Until Messiah the Prince, There shall be seven weeks and sixty-two weeks; The street shall be built again, and the wall, Even in troublesome times.

26 "And after the sixty-two weeks Messiah shall be cut off, but not for Himself; And the people of the prince who is to come Shall destroy the city and the sanctuary. The end of it shall be with a flood, And till the end of the war desolations are determined.

27 Then he shall confirm a covenant with many for

**Messiah shall be cut off** (v. 26)—"Cut off" was a common reference to death.

**Then** (v. 27)—This is clearly the end of the age, the Second Advent judgment, because the bringing in of righteousness did not occur seven years after the death of Messiah, nor did the destruction of Jerusalem fit the seven-year period (occurring 37 years later). This is the future seven-year period that ends with sin's final judgment and Christ's reign of righteousness.

**he shall confirm** (v. 27)—literally, "he causes to prevail, "he" being the last mentioned prince (v. 26), leader of the Roman sphere, the Antichrist; this refers to a seven-year covenant or pact with Israel that will turn out to be shorter

**one week** (v. 27)—the final seven years that will be the time of Antichrist

**middle of the week** (v. 27)—the halfway point of the seven years or 70th week; the Antichrist will break his pact with Israel, which will have by then resumed its ancient sacrificial system

**abominations . . . one who makes desolate** (v. 27)—This violation of the holy temple and the honoring of God's presence will ruin all that the Jews hold sacred.

**the consummation** (v. 27)—God permits this tribulation under the Antichrist's persecutions and ultimately triumphs, achieving judgment of the sin and sinners in Israel and the world.

*one week; But in the middle of the week He shall bring an end to sacrifice and offering. And on the wing of abominations shall be one who makes desolate, Even until the consummation, which is determined, Is poured out on the desolate."*

# Understanding the Text

4) What motivated Daniel to pray so intensely (see 9:1–2)? Describe his intercession, his manner of approaching God. What ingredients do you see? What was his tone?

_____

_____

_____

_____

5) Summarize the answer to Daniel's prayer as revealed by the angel Gabriel (that is, the prophecy of the 70 weeks). What do all these numbers mean?

_____

_____

_____

_____

6) What does chapter 9 say about the Antichrist? How is he described?

_____

_____

_____

_____

_____

(verses to consider: Mark 13:14; 2 Thessalonians 2:3–10; Revelation 13:1–10)

# Cross Reference

Read the following verses from Matthew 21.

1 Now when they drew near Jerusalem, and came to Bethphage, at the Mount of Olives, then Jesus sent two disciples,

2 saying to them, "Go into the village opposite you, and immediately you will find a donkey tied, and a colt with her. Loose them and bring them to Me.

3 "And if anyone says anything to you, you shall say, 'The Lord has need of them,' and immediately he will send them."

4 All this was done that it might be fulfilled which was spoken by the prophet, saying:

5 "Tell the daughter of Zion, 'Behold, your King is coming to you, Lowly, and sitting on a donkey, A colt, the foal of a donkey.' "

6 So the disciples went and did as Jesus commanded them.

7 They brought the donkey and the colt, laid their clothes on them, and set Him on them.

8 And a very great multitude spread their clothes on the road; others cut down branches from the trees and spread them on the road.

9 Then the multitudes who went before and those who followed cried out, saying: "Hosanna to the Son of David! 'Blessed is He who comes in the name of the LORD!' Hosanna in the highest!"

10 And when He had come into Jerusalem, all the city was moved, saying, "Who is this?"

11 So the multitudes said, "This is Jesus, the prophet from Nazareth of Galilee."

# Exploring the Meaning

7) What does the triumphal entry of Christ into Jerusalem as recorded by Matthew have to do with 9:25?

_____

_____

_____

_____

_____

8) Read Numbers 14:11–19. How does Moses's intercession for his people compare or contrast with the intercession of Daniel as recorded in chapter 9?

_____

_____

_____

_____

_____

9) Read Revelation 19:19–21. What does this reveal about the future of the Antichrist?

_____

_____

_____

_____

_____

_____

## Summing Up . . .

"People have a natural longing for a better day, a time of peace and harmony among nations, of greater economic stability, and of decreased crime, disease, and discord. But Scripture is clear that, despite temporary times of improvement, things are destined to become much worse before they permanently become better. Human society faces a time that is going to be more calamitous than any ever experienced before. . . . It will mark the end of humanity's day and the coming of God's." —*John MacArthur*

## Reflecting on the Text

10) What would you say to the person who asserts that the world will get better and better as technology advances and as governments band together to fight both natural and human-made problems?

_____

_____

_____

_____

_____

_____

11) How well do you understand end times prophecy? What questions do you have? What details are still unclear in your mind? Take one question a day and study until you feel you have a grasp of what the Bible teaches. (Note: John MacArthur's New Testament Commentary on Matthew 24–28, pages 1–126, provides a detailed explanation of what Jesus taught about the events surrounding His Second Coming.)

_____

_____

_____

_____

_____

12) As you ponder Daniel's prayer in this chapter, what example or encouragement can you glean for your own prayer life? How can you improve your prayer habits?

_____

_____

_____

_____

_____

_____

# Recording Your Thoughts

_____

_____

_____

_____

_____

_____

_____

_____

_____

_____

_____

_____

_____

_____

_____

_____

_____

_____

_____

_____

## For further study, see the following passages:

| | | |
|---|---|---|
| Leviticus 25:4–5 | Deuteronomy 28:1–14 | 1 Kings 9:3 |
| 2 Chronicles 36:21 | Ezra 9:5 | Nehemiah 2:1–8 |
| Psalm 75:6–7 | Jeremiah 25:11–12, 31 | Zechariah 13:1 |
| Matthew 13:41–43 | Matthew 24:21 | 2 Thessalonians 2:4 |
| Hebrews 9:26 | Revelation 11:2–3 | |

# Prophecies Concerning Persia and Greece

Daniel 10:1—11:4

## Opening Thought

1) Many churches emphasize the activity of demons, and believers are commonly heard praying against "the spirit of _____" or "a spirit of _____." Special prayer conferences may be held in which guest speakers teach about territorial spirits, spiritual warfare, even exorcism.

What do you think of all this? Is this a biblical practice? How much attention should believers devote to the subject of spiritual warfare?

_____

_____

_____

_____

_____

_____

_____

_____

_____

_____

_____

_____

# Background of the Passage

Captured as a young man and taken from his homeland far away to Babylon (1:1–7), Daniel became God's ambassador to rich and powerful world leaders. For most of his life, this humble prophet carried out a quiet but effective ministry behind the scenes, yet much of it took place on the international stage.

Not only was Daniel a powerful example (in his steadfast devotion to God and his refusal to capitulate to pagan beliefs or practices—1:8–21; 6:1–28), and a man of prayer (2:16–23; 6:10–13; 9:3–19), but he also was a bold and powerful truth-teller (2:24–49; 4:19–26; 5:13–31).

The Book of Daniel, however, is not first and foremost a biography; it is apocalyptic literature. The Greek word *apokalypsis*, from which the English term "apocalypse" is derived, means "an unveiling, disclosing, or revelation." Thus, while the entire Bible is revelation from God, the Book of Daniel is unique in both the content of its revelation and the manner in which it was disclosed.

Through visions filled with strange sights and symbols, God gave Daniel a panoramic and long-term view of the future. World empires (and their destinies) are described (2:1—7:28), and the restoration of Israel (both immediate and ultimate) is explained (8:1—12:13).

The beginning of chapter 10 has Daniel still in Babylon (though many of the Jewish exiles had begun to return to their homeland following the decree of Cyrus). The rebuilding of the temple was underway. The nation seemed to be at peace, and the future looked bright. Daniel experienced a vision of a glorious man, however, who revealed that Israel's peace and freedom would not last. In the process, Daniel also learned about conflict in the spiritual realm.

# Bible Passage

Read 10:1—11:4, noting the key words and definitions to the right of the passage.

## Daniel 10:1—11:4

¹ *In the third year of Cyrus king of Persia a message was revealed to Daniel, whose name was*

**third year** (v. 1)—536 B.C.; two years had passed since the decree of Cyrus to let Israel return to her homeland

called Belteshazzar. The message was true, but the appointed time was long; and he understood the message, and had understanding of the vision.

2 In those days I, Daniel, was mourning three full weeks.

3 I ate no pleasant food, no meat or wine came into my mouth, nor did I anoint myself at all, till three whole weeks were fulfilled.

4 Now on the twenty-fourth day of the first month, as I was by the side of the great river, that is, the Tigris,

5 I lifted my eyes and looked, and behold, a certain man clothed in linen, whose waist was girded with gold of Uphaz!

6 His body was like beryl, his face like the appearance of lightning, his eyes like torches of fire, his arms and feet like burnished bronze in color, and the sound of his words like the voice of a multitude.

7 And I, Daniel, alone saw the vision, for the men who were with me did not see the vision; but a great terror fell upon them, so that they fled to hide themselves.

8 Therefore I was left alone when I saw this great vision, and no strength remained in me; for my vigor was turned to frailty in me, and I retained no strength.

9 Yet I heard the sound of his words; and while I heard the sound of his words I was in a deep sleep on my face, with my face to the ground.

10 Suddenly, a hand touched me, which made me tremble on my knees and on the palms of my hands.

11 And he said to me, "O Daniel, man greatly beloved, understand the words that I speak to you, and stand upright, for I have now been sent to you." While he was speaking this word to me, I stood trembling.

12 Then he said to me, "Do not fear, Daniel, for

**a certain man** (v. 5)—The messenger whom Daniel saw was distinct from the angel Michael, from whom he needed assistance (verse 13). The glory described by Daniel has led many to believe this was Christ in a pre-incarnate form.

**His body . . . like beryl** (v. 6)—an almost identical description to the one of Christ found in Revelation 1:13–14

**my vigor turned to frailty** (v. 8)—a common response during human encounters with heavenly visitors

**a hand touched me** (v. 10)—Most likely this was Gabriel, who interpreted other visions to Daniel (see 8:16; 9:20–23).

**your words were heard** (v. 12)—a great encouragement from God who was attentive to prayer and acted to answer

**prince of . . . Persia . . . twenty-one days** (v. 13)—This three week delay was due to an evil angel opposing Gabriel in heavenly warfare. This angel was especially anointed with Persian power in an effort to thwart the work of God. Satan engages in heavenly warfare to influence generations and nations against God and His people.

**Michael** (v. 13)—the chief angel of heaven (see 10:21; 12:1), Michael remained to assure that the Jews would be free to return to their land

**many days yet to come** (v. 14)—a reference to the future plan of God for His people, extending from Daniel's time to that of the Antichrist

**was strengthened** (v. 19)—This was the third time (see verses 10 and 16), showing the

from the first day that you set your heart to understand, and to humble yourself before your God, your words were heard; and I have come because of your words.

13 "But the prince of the kingdom of Persia withstood me twenty-one days; and behold, Michael, one of the chief princes, came to help me, for I had been left alone there with the kings of Persia.

14 "Now I have come to make you understand what will happen to your people in the latter days, for the vision refers to many days yet to come."

15 When he had spoken such words to me, I turned my face toward the ground and became speechless.

16 And suddenly, one having the likeness of the sons of men touched my lips; then I opened my mouth and spoke, saying to him who stood before me, "My lord, because of the vision my sorrows have overwhelmed me, and I have retained no strength.

17 "For how can this servant of my lord talk with you, my lord? As for me, no strength remains in me now, nor is any breath left in me."

18 Then again, the one having the likeness of a man touched me and strengthened me.

19 And he said, "O man greatly beloved, fear not! Peace be to you; be strong, yes, be strong!" So when he spoke to me I was strengthened, and said, "Let my lord speak, for you have strengthened me."

20 Then he said, "Do you know why I have come to you? And now I must return to fight with the prince of Persia; and when I have gone forth, indeed the prince of Greece will come.

21 "But I will tell you what is noted in the Scripture of Truth. (No one upholds me against these, except Michael your prince.

11:1 "Also in the first year of Darius the Mede, I, even I, stood up to confirm and strengthen him.)

2 "And now I will tell you the truth: Behold, three

overwhelming trauma of divine presence and revelation.

**prince of Greece** (v. 20)—an evil angel contesting for the kingdom of Greece

**Scripture of Truth** (v. 21)—God's plan of certain and true designs for men and nations, which He can reveal according to His discretion (see 11:2)

**except Michael** (v. 21)—The angel with Michael intended to handle the demons of Persia and Greece; this actually forms the heavenly basis for the earthly unfolding of history in 11:2–35.

**first year** (11:1)—539 B.C.

**I, stood up to . . . strengthen him** (v. 1)—The messenger of 10:10–14. continued to speak of assisting Michael (even as Michael had strengthened him in the battle with demons in 10:21), confirming Darius in his purposes of kindness to Israel in decreeing their return.

**And now I will tell you the truth** (v. 2.)—This section unfolds the near fulfillment of the Persian kingdom and the reign of Greece through Antiochus Epiphanes.

**three more kings . . . and the fourth** (v. 2)—The three Persian rulers after Cyrus were Cambyses (530–522 B.C.), Pseudo-Smerdis (522 B.C.), and Darius I Hystapes (522–486 B.C.). The fourth is Xerxes I, called Ahasuerus in Esther.

**a mighty king** (v. 3)—Alexander the Great

*more kings will arise in Persia, and the fourth shall be far richer than them all; by his strength, through his riches, he shall stir up all against the realm of Greece.*

3 *"Then a mighty king shall arise, who shall rule with great dominion, and do according to his will.*

4 *"And when he has arisen, his kingdom shall be broken up and divided toward the four winds of heaven, but not among his posterity nor according to his dominion with which he ruled; for his kingdom shall be uprooted, even for others besides these.*

# Understanding the Text

2) How did Daniel describe the "man" he encountered by the Tigris? What was his appearance? His demeanor?

_____

_____

_____

_____

_____

3) Why did the "man" say that he had been delayed in bringing Daniel an answer to his prayers?

_____

_____

_____

_____

_____

4) What was revealed to Daniel about the immediate future? What is the "Scripture of Truth"?

_____

_____

_____

_____

_____

_____

## Cross Reference

Consider this passage from Ephesians 6.

10 *Finally, my brethren, be strong in the Lord and in the power of His might.*

11 *Put on the whole armor of God, that you may be able to stand against the wiles of the devil.*

12 *For we do not wrestle against flesh and blood, but against principalities, against powers, against the rulers of the darkness of this age, against spiritual hosts of wickedness in the heavenly places.*

13 *Therefore take up the whole armor of God, that you may be able to withstand in the evil day, and having done all, to stand.*

14 *Stand therefore, having girded your waist with truth, having put on the breastplate of righteousness,*

15 *and having shod your feet with the preparation of the gospel of peace;*

16 *above all, taking the shield of faith with which you will be able to quench all the fiery darts of the wicked one.*

17 *And take the helmet of salvation, and the sword of the Spirit, which is the word of God;*

18 *praying always with all prayer and supplication in the Spirit, being watchful to this end with all perseverance and supplication for all the saints—*

## Exploring the Meaning

5) How does this passage clarify or illuminate the events described in chapter 10?

_____

_____

_____

_____

_____

6) Daniel mentions his habit of fasting (10:2–3). What is the purpose of this discipline?

_____

_____

_____

_____

(verses to consider: Nehemiah 1:4; Psalm 35:13; Matthew 17:21; Luke 2:37; 5:33; Acts 13:2; 14:23; see also Matthew 6:17 and Luke 5:33–35)

7) In the midst of his divine encounter, Daniel reported feeling weak (perhaps emotionally, spiritually, and physically). Verse 18 speaks of the "man" touching Daniel. What do you think this involved? When have you sensed the unmistakable touch of God on your own life (and a supernatural imparting of strength)? What happened?

_____

_____

_____

_____

_____

_____

_____

# Summing Up . . .

"One of Satan's most effective strategies, and therefore one of a believer's greatest dangers, is the delusion that no seriously threatening conflict between good and evil is really raging in the invisible and supernatural realm. After all, it is argued, there appear to be so many good things in the world today. Numerous ancient evils, such as slavery and race hatred, have disappeared or improved dramatically. People have never been so concerned about getting along together, understanding one another, and working with one another to improve individual lives and society as a whole. . . .

"That sort of thinking not only is naïve but inevitably leads to lethargy, indifference, indolence, and spiritual stagnation. A biblical perspective on the situation and a clear perception of the direction things are really moving— especially in light of Scripture's teaching about the end times—does not leave room for such delusion in the mind of any believer. The war between God and Satan has not diminished but intensified, and so has its front on this earth."
—John MacArthur

# Reflecting on the Text

8) As you read of the spiritual warfare taking place behind the scenes in chapter 10, how are you motivated to pray differently this week?

_____

_____

_____

_____

_____

_____

_____

_____

_____

9) Daniel is portrayed time and again in this book as a man of deep spiritual intensity and devotion. He constantly is seen praying and seeking after God. How does his example challenge and motivate you? What's the secret to having such a passionate hunger for God?

_____

_____

_____

_____

_____

_____

_____

_____

10) Daniel spoke of overwhelming sorrows (verse 16). In response to this admission, he experienced a divine touch. What trials or difficulties are overwhelming you? Express the cry of your heart to God and ask for His compassionate touch.

_____

_____

_____

_____

_____

_____

_____

_____

_____

# Recording Your Thoughts

_____

_____

_____

_____

_____

_____

_____

_____

_____

_____

_____

_____

_____

_____

_____

_____

_____

_____

_____

_____

_____

_____

_____

## For further study, see the following passages:

| | | |
|---|---|---|
| Joshua 5:13–15 | Judges 6:11–23 | Ezra 1:1 |
| Isaiah 46:9–11 | Daniel 8:3–9 | Jude 9 |
| Revelation 1:17 | Revelation 12:7 | Revelation 16:12–14 |

# The Warring Kings of the North and South

## Opening Thought

1) What would you say and do if a close friend or family member began to be enamored with his or her horoscope and began to spend a lot of money calling telephone psychics?

Why are these vague and often wrong seers so popular and so often consulted by millions? What is behind this growing trend?

_____

_____

_____

_____

_____

_____

_____

_____

_____

_____

_____

_____

_____

_____

_____

# Background of the Passage

In chapter 11, the Spirit of God continued to reveal to the prophet Daniel advance glimpses of both Israel's humiliation and restoration. This prophetic passage (as with 8:3–26) sweeps all the way from the history of spiritual conflict in Israel (11:5–35) to the tribulation (verses 36–42) when Michael aids in fully delivering Israel (see 12:1). The prophecy looks ahead from Daniel to the final Antichrist.

The death of Alexander the Great resulted in a twenty-two-year-long power struggle for control of the Grecian Empire. Eventually four generals assumed rule over four sectors of the empire. Even then the hostilities continued. The bulk of this chapter focuses on a yet-future, long-running conflict between "the king of the South" (verse 5), that is, the Ptolemies (rulers of Egypt and Arabia) and "the king of the North," that is, the Seleucians (rulers of Syria and Babylonia).

The detail of this pre-written history is so minute and accurate and confirmed by history that unbelieving, rationalistic critics have, without evidence, insisted it must have been written four hundred years later than Daniel, after it all had occurred. This, of course, is not only an attack on the inspiration of Scripture, but a charge which would make the author a deceiver.

Christians know that it is nothing for an omniscient, omnipotent, and sovereign God to reveal the course of future world events. And given the 100 percent accuracy of the prophecies concerning events two to three hundred years in the future (that is, the revelations about events in the Grecian Empire), it is wise to study carefully what was revealed to Daniel about things yet to come.

# Bible Passage

Read 11:5–45, noting the key words and definitions to the right of the passage.

**Daniel 11:5–45**

5 *"Also the king of the South shall become strong, as well as one of his princes; and he shall gain power over him and have dominion. His dominion shall be a great dominion.*

*king of the South* (v. 5)—the Ptolemies, leaders of Egypt

*king of the North* (v. 6)—Seleucians, rulers of Syria; these territories/peoples (identified by

6 *"And at the end of some years they shall join forces, for the daughter of the king of the South shall go to the king of the North to make an agreement; but she shall not retain the power of her authority, and neither he nor his authority shall stand; but she shall be given up, with those who brought her, and with him who begot her, and with him who strengthened her in those times.*

7 *"But from a branch of her roots one shall arise in his place, who shall come with an army, enter the fortress of the king of the North, and deal with them and prevail.*

8 *"And he shall also carry their gods captive to Egypt, with their princes and their precious articles of silver and gold; and he shall continue more years than the king of the North.*

9 *"Also the king of the North shall come to the kingdom of the king of the South, but shall return to his own land.*

10 *"However his sons shall stir up strife, and assemble a multitude of great forces; and one shall certainly come and overwhelm and pass through; then he shall return to his fortress and stir up strife.*

11 *"And the king of the South shall be moved with rage, and go out and fight with him, with the king of the North, who shall muster a great multitude; but the multitude shall be given into the hand of his enemy.*

12 *"When he has taken away the multitude, his heart will be lifted up; and he will cast down tens of thousands, but he will not prevail.*

13 *"For the king of the North will return and muster a multitude greater than the former, and shall certainly come at the end of some years with a great army and much equipment.*

14 *"Now in those times many shall rise up against the king of the South. Also, violent men of your*

their geographical location to Palestine) fought for almost two hundred years

**join forces** (v. 6)—Berenice, daughter of Egypt's Ptolemy II Philadephus (285–246 B.C.), married Syria's King Antiochus II Theos (261–246 B.C.) who divorced his wife to marry Berenice. Later, that divorced wife murdered Berenice, her baby son, and even Antiochus.

**from a branch of her roots** (v. 7)—The murdered Berenice's brother stood in his father's place; this was Ptolemy III Euergetes of Egypt (246–222 B.C.) who conquered Syria, looting their great treasure (v. 8).

**king of the North shall come** (v. 9)—Syria's Callinicus attacked Egypt in 240 B.C. but retreated, soundly beaten.

**his sons** (v. 10)—Seleucus's sons (successors) kept up war against Egypt as described in verses 11–35.

**king of the South** (v. 11)—Ptolemy IV Philopator (222–203 B.C.) devastated the Syrian army under Antiochus III the Great (223–187 B.C.); this Egyptian advantage would be brief (verse 12).

**king of the North** (vv. 13–16)—Thirteen years later Antiochus returned with a great army, and in a series of strikes against Egypt brought Palestine ("the Glorious Land") into his control as far south as Gaza.

**violent men of your people** (v. 14)—Violent Jews wanted independence from Egypt but failed in their revolt.

**he who comes against him** (v. 16)—Antiochus III the Great took lasting dominion over Israel.

people shall exalt themselves in fulfillment of the vision, but they shall fall.

15 "So the king of the North shall come and build a siege mound, and take a fortified city; and the forces of the South shall not withstand him. Even his choice troops shall have no strength to resist.

16 "But he who comes against him shall do according to his own will, and no one shall stand against him. He shall stand in the Glorious Land with destruction in his power.

17 "He shall also set his face to enter with the strength of his whole kingdom, and upright ones with him; thus shall he do. And he shall give him the daughter of women to destroy it; but she shall not stand with him, or be for him.

18 "After this he shall turn his face to the coastlands, and shall take many. But a ruler shall bring the reproach against them to an end; and with the reproach removed, he shall turn back on him.

19 "Then he shall turn his face toward the fortress of his own land; but he shall stumble and fall, and not be found.

20 "There shall arise in his place one who imposes taxes on the glorious kingdom; but within a few days he shall be destroyed, but not in anger or in battle.

21 "And in his place shall arise a vile person, to whom they will not give the honor of royalty; but he shall come in peaceably, and seize the kingdom by intrigue.

22 "With the force of a flood they shall be swept away from before him and be broken, and also the prince of the covenant.

23 "And after the league is made with him he shall act deceitfully, for he shall come up and become strong with a small number of people.

24 "He shall enter peaceably, even into the richest places of the province; and he shall do what his fathers have not done, nor his forefathers: he

**give . . . the daughter** (v. 17) —Antiochus, feeling pressure from Rome to make peace with Egypt, offered his daughter Cleopatra to marry Ptolemy V Epiphanes (192 B.C.). The Syrian hoped that his daughter would spy in order to help him "destroy" or weaken Egypt and bring it under his power. Cleopatra, instead of helping her father, favored her Egyptian mate.

**a ruler** (v. 18)—The Roman Lucius Scipio Asiaticus defeated Antiochus (191–190 B.C.).

**fall** (v. 19)—Antiochus returned from defeat to his own land compelled by Rome to relinquish all his territory west of the Taurus and to repay the costs of war. He was likely killed by defenders of a Persian temple that he tried to plunder at night in Elymais.

**one who imposes taxes** (v. 20)—Increasingly powerful Rome required Seleucus IV Philopator to render tribute; he in turn tried to tax his subjects.

**a vile person** (v. 21)—Seleucid came to the throne when his brother Seleucus was murdered. The most cruel king of the North, he was known as Antiochus IV Epiphanes.

**they shall be swept away** (v. 22)—Egypt's armies were swept away by Antiochus's invading forces as by a flood. Israel's "prince of the covenant," Onias III, was murdered by his own defecting brother Menelaus at the request of Antiochus (171 B.C.).

**the league** (v. 23)—Antiochus's alliance with Ptolemy VI Philometer, a deceitful plot to gain greater power in Egypt

**enter peaceably** (v. 24)—Under the guise of friendship, Antiochus

shall disperse among them the plunder, spoil, and riches; and he shall devise his plans against the strongholds, but only for a time.

25 "He shall stir up his power and his courage against the king of the South with a great army. And the king of the South shall be stirred up to battle with a very great and mighty army; but he shall not stand, for they shall devise plans against him.

26 "Yes, those who eat of the portion of his delicacies shall destroy him; his army shall be swept away, and many shall fall down slain.

27 "Both these kings' hearts shall be bent on evil, and they shall speak lies at the same table; but it shall not prosper, for the end will still be at the appointed time.

28 "While returning to his land with great riches, his heart shall be moved against the holy covenant; so he shall do damage and return to his own land.

29 "At the appointed time he shall return and go toward the south; but it shall not be like the former or the latter.

30 "For ships from Cyprus shall come against him; therefore he shall be grieved, and return in rage against the holy covenant, and do damage. So he shall return and show regard for those who forsake the holy covenant.

31 "And forces shall be mustered by him, and they shall defile the sanctuary fortress; then they shall take away the daily sacrifices, and place there the abomination of desolation.

32 "Those who do wickedly against the covenant he shall corrupt with flattery; but the people who know their God shall be strong, and carry out great exploits.

33 "And those of the people who understand shall instruct many; yet for many days they shall fall by sword and flame, by captivity and plundering.

34 "Now when they fall, they shall be aided with a

plundered the riches of Egypt; to gain support he gave lavish gifts.

**his power . . . against the . . . South** (v. 25)—Antiochus attacked Philometer; the latter fell due to treachery by supporters.

**those who eat** (v. 26)— Betraying counselors, whom Philometer fed, encouraged him to attack Syria, thus securing his defeat.

**shall speak lies** (v. 27)— Antiochus pretended to help to reinstate Ptolemy Philometer to Egypt's throne, occupied then by Ptolemy Euergetes. Both kings lied at the conference, and Antiochus set Philometer up as king at Memphis, whereas Euergetes reigned at Alexandria.

**against the holy covenant** (v. 28)—Antiochus, en route north through Israel, met a revolt and struck Jerusalem's temple. The results were catastrophic: eighty thousand dead, forty thousand captured, and the sacrificial system profaned.

**toward the south** (v. 29)—a third (unsuccessful) invasion of Egypt by Antiochus (168 B.C.)

**ships . . . come against him** (v. 30)—A Roman fleet from Cyprus sided with Egypt, thwarting Antiochus's attack. Antiochus retreated, taking out his rage on the Israelites in his path.

**defile the sanctuary** (v. 31)— Worship was halted, people were slaughtered, a pig was even sacrificed on the altar, and a statue of the Olympian god Zeus was erected.

**abomination of desolation** (v. 31)—The spreading of sow's broth on the altar and ban on sacrifices were only a preview of the

little help; but many shall join with them by intrigue.

35 "And some of those of understanding shall fall, to refine them, purify them, and make them white, until the time of the end; because it is still for the appointed time.

36 "Then the king shall do according to his own will: he shall exalt and magnify himself above every god, shall speak blasphemies against the God of gods, and shall prosper till the wrath has been accomplished; for what has been determined shall be done.

37 "He shall regard neither the God of his fathers nor the desire of women, nor regard any god; for he shall exalt himself above them all.

38 "But in their place he shall honor a god of fortresses; and a god which his fathers did not know he shall honor with gold and silver, with precious stones and pleasant things.

39 "Thus he shall act against the strongest fortresses with a foreign god, which he shall acknowledge, and advance its glory; and he shall cause them to rule over many, and divide the land for gain.

40 "At the time of the end the king of the South shall attack him; and the king of the North shall come against him like a whirlwind, with chariots, horsemen, and with many ships; and he shall enter the countries, overwhelm them, and pass through.

41 "He shall also enter the Glorious Land, and many countries shall be overthrown; but these shall escape from his hand: Edom, Moab, and the prominent people of Ammon.

42 "He shall stretch out his hand against the countries, and the land of Egypt shall not escape.

43 "He shall have power over the treasures of gold and silver, and over all the precious things of Egypt; also the Libyans and Ethiopians shall follow at his heels.

44 "But news from the east and the north shall trou-

abomination that will happen under Antichrist.

**Those who do wickedly** (v. 32–34)—the Jews who aided and abetted Antiochus

**the people who know their God** (v. 32)—The Jews loyal to God (called Hasideans) suffered death rather than compromise; Judas Maccabeus eventually led them in a successful revolt.

**instruct many** (v. 33)—Jews who "cause to be wise"; that is, they know and believe the truth and instruct others in the way

**to refine them** (v. 35)—The gracious design of persecution and martyrdom was (and is) to sanctify true believers.

**time of the end . . . appointed time** (v. 35)—a forward leap across thousands of years of history from Antiochus to a future similar trial

**Then** (v. 36)—This points to the future "time of the end," the far fulfillment of God's prophetic plan. Here are the details of Daniel's seventieth week. Antiochus Epiphanes is the perfect transition point to the actual Antichrist.

**God of his fathers** (v. 37)—The word for "God" is *elohim*, a word that is plural, thus, in the context, probably "gods."

**desire of women** (v. 37)—This could mean that Antichrist will be a homosexual; it surely means that he has no interest in women, for example, as one who is celibate.

**god of fortresses** (v. 38)—The term for fortress means "a strong place"; power will be the god of Antichrist and he will use all his treasure to become more powerful and to finance wars.

*ble him; therefore he shall go out with great fury to destroy and annihilate many.*

45 *"And he shall plant the tents of his palace between the seas and the glorious holy mountain; yet he shall come to his end, and no one will help him.*

**king of . . . South . . . North** (v. 40)—Here is the final north versus south conflict, during the time of Antichrist.

**news** (v. 44)—Military bulletins alert the willful king of other sectors of the world deploying troops to the Palestinian theater.

**his end** (v. 45)—No one will be able to help this willful king/Antichrist against God when He, by the return of Christ, brings him to his end.

# *Understanding the Text*

2) What happened immediately following the death of the mighty king mentioned in 11:3?

_____

_____

_____

_____

_____

_____

3) Who is the "vile person" mentioned in 11:21 and why is he described in this way?

_____

_____

_____

_____

_____

_____

4) What did Daniel observe happening when the northern king was opposed by ships from Cyprus (that is, Rome; see verses 29–35) and was forced to retreat? How did he react? What were the different responses of the people of "the holy covenant" to this invading king?

_____

_____

_____

_____

_____

# Cross Reference

Read this passage from Revelation 19.

11 *Now I saw heaven opened, and behold, a white horse. And He who sat on him was called Faithful and True, and in righteousness He judges and makes war.*

12 *His eyes were like a flame of fire, and on His head were many crowns. He had a name written that no one knew except Himself.*

13 *He was clothed with a robe dipped in blood, and His name is called The Word of God.*

14 *And the armies in heaven, clothed in fine linen, white and clean, followed Him on white horses.*

15 *Now out of His mouth goes a sharp sword, that with it He should strike the nations. And He Himself will rule them with a rod of iron. He Himself treads the winepress of the fierceness and wrath of Almighty God.*

16 *And He has on His robe and on His thigh a name written: KING OF KINGS AND LORD OF LORDS.*

17 *Then I saw an angel standing in the sun; and he cried with a loud voice, saying to all the birds that fly in the midst of heaven, "Come and gather together for the supper of the great God,*

18 *"that you may eat the flesh of kings, the flesh of captains, the flesh of mighty men, the flesh of horses and of those who sit on them, and the flesh of all people, free and slave, both small and great."*

19 *And I saw the beast, the kings of the earth, and their armies, gathered together to make war against Him who sat on the horse and against His army.*

20 *Then the beast was captured, and with him the false prophet who worked signs in his presence, by which he deceived those who received the mark of the beast and those who worshiped his image. These two were cast alive into the lake of fire burning with brimstone.*

21 *And the rest were killed with the sword which proceeded from the mouth of Him who sat on the horse. And all the birds were filled with their flesh.*

## *Exploring the Meaning*

5) In what ways does Revelation 19:11–21 echo the message of 11:36–45?

_____

_____

_____

_____

_____

6) What is the meaning of the phrase "the people who know their God shall . . . carry out great exploits" (verse 32)?

_____

_____

_____

_____

_____

7) Read Romans 5:3–5. Then recall that 11:35 speaks of the refining effects of persecution and martyrdom. How is this so?

_____

_____

_____

_____

# Summing Up . . .

"In modern times the church (at least in the West) has rarely faced physical persecution. Satan's attacks have become much more subtle-the type of attack detailed, for example, in C. S. Lewis's *The Screwtape Letters*. Instead of threatening the body, Satan's persecutions today aim at the ego. They threaten our selfish pride, need for acceptance, or status. Satan has largely destroyed the spiritual effectiveness of the church without having to kill the individual believers in it. In fact, letting believers live self-centered, complacent, indolent, worldly lives is more effective in keeping people from being attracted to the Christian faith than killing them. Martyrs are respected for the strength of their character; compromisers are despised." —*John MacArthur*

# Reflecting on the Text

8) Had you been living as a Jew during the time of Antiochus Epiphanes' onslaught, how do you think you would have fared in the face of persecution? Why?

_____

_____

_____

_____

9) How (practically and specifically) can you deepen your faith and devotion to Christ so that you are prepared for attacks (whether overt or subtle) against your faith?

_____

_____

_____

_____

_____

_____

10) Meditate on 11:32b. In the context this refers, of course, to those during the time of Antiochus. But the underlying principle is valid for all times: Those who walk intimately with God will be marked by lives of powerful faith. What great exploits are you willing to trust God for this week? How can you step out in faith and, following the lead of the Holy Spirit, serve God more effectively?

_____

_____

_____

_____

_____

_____

## *Recording Your Thoughts*

_____

_____

_____

_____

_____

_____

_____

_____

_____

_____

_____

## For further study, see the following passages:

Daniel 7:8–26

Daniel 8:3–12, 23–26

Daniel 10:20–21

Zechariah 12:2–3

Zechariah 14:2–3

Revelation 9:16

Revelation 16:12

Revelation 19:17–21

# The End Times

## *Opening Thought*

1) If Daniel were given a vision of our society and its future, what major weaknesses and strengths do you think would be identified? Why? What do you think will happen in and to this country in the coming years?

_____

_____

_____

_____

_____

_____

_____

_____

_____

_____

_____

_____

_____

_____

_____

_____

_____

# Background of the Passage

The Book of Daniel was written to encourage those Jews living in exile in Babylonia. Though their past had been filled with much heartbreak and pain, and though they faced certain difficulty in the future, Daniel's vision gave the Jews numerous reasons for hope: (1) it revealed God as the sovereign Lord who controls the universe; (2) it showed that God had a program for His people Israel during and after a long period of Gentile domination; (3) it served as a reminder that persecution and suffering will not last indefinitely; (4) it revealed that God is faithful so he keeps His covenant promises; (5) it declared that preservation and ultimate restoration are the destiny of the people of God.

In the final vision which became the final chapter of his apocalyptic book, Daniel was reassured that though the Great Tribulation will be a time of unparalleled distress, Israel (as a nation) will be delivered by the angelic prince Michael. The concerned prophet was further consoled by the promise that Jews who lose their lives at the hands of the Gentiles will be resurrected. These closing verses reveal many other specifics about the end times; Daniel probably did not comprehended these details. Certainly he did not live to see them fulfilled.

Nevertheless, Daniel lived close to God all the days of his life, serving Him faithfully and with great integrity. For that unswerving devotion he will receive a glorious reward (12:12–13). That is also the hope of every modern-day saint who trusts and obeys the Lord Jesus Christ-the opportunity to share in the blessings of His millennial and eternal kingdoms.

# Bible Passage

Read 12:1–13, noting the key words and definitions to the right of the passage.

**Daniel 12:1–13**

¹ *"At that time Michael shall stand up, The great prince who stands watch over the sons of your people; And there shall be a time of trouble, Such as never was since there was a nation, Even to*

**that time** (v. 1)—This points back to 11:36–45, the time of the ascendancy of Antichrist during the final tribulation period. During that period, Michael the archangel of 10:13 and 21 ministers with special attention to protecting Israel during that Gentile time.

*that time. And at that time your people shall be delivered, Every one who is found written in the book.*

2 *And many of those who sleep in the dust of the earth shall awake, Some to everlasting life, Some to shame and everlasting contempt.*

3 *Those who are wise shall shine Like the brightness of the firmament, And those who turn many to righteousness Like the stars forever and ever.*

4 *"But you, Daniel, shut up the words, and seal the book until the time of the end; many shall run to and fro, and knowledge shall increase."*

5 *Then I, Daniel, looked; and there stood two others, one on this riverbank and the other on that riverbank.*

6 *And one said to the man clothed in linen, who was above the waters of the river, "How long shall the fulfillment of these wonders be?"*

7 *Then I heard the man clothed in linen, who was above the waters of the river, when he held up his right hand and his left hand to heaven, and swore by Him who lives forever, that it shall be for a time, times, and half a time; and when the power of the holy people has been completely shattered, all these things shall be finished.*

8 *Although I heard, I did not understand. Then I said, "My lord, what shall be the end of these things?"*

9 *And he said, "Go your way, Daniel, for the words are closed up and sealed till the time of the end.*

10 *"Many shall be purified, made white, and refined, but the wicked shall do wickedly; and none of the wicked shall understand, but the wise shall understand.*

11 *"And from the time that the daily sacrifice is taken away, and the abomination of desolation is set up, there shall be one thousand two hundred and ninety days.*

12 *"Blessed is he who waits, and comes to the one thousand three hundred and thirty-five days.*

**your people** (v. 1)—Daniel's Israelite brethren who can have hope even in the unprecedented distress set for the Great Tribulation

**written in the book** (v. 1)—the book of the saved (see Revelation 20:12, 15; 21:27)

**many . . . Some . . . Some** (v. 2)—Two groups will arise from death, constituting the "many," meaning all, as in John 5:29. Those of faith will arise to eternal life, the rest of the unsaved to eternal torment. The souls of Old Testament saints are already with the Lord; at this time they will receive glorified bodies.

**wise** (v. 3)—those having true knowledge, by faith in God's Word, not only leaders (as in 11:33), but others (11:35; 12:10)

**shall shine** (v. 3)—To shine in glory is a privilege of all the saved. The faithfulness of the believer's life and witness will determine his or her eternal capacity to reflect God's glory.

**the time of the end** (v. 4)—a reference to the seventieth week of tribulation (see 11:35 and 40)

**run to and fro** (v. 4)—This Hebrews verb form always refers to the movement of a person searching for something. In the tribulation, people will search for answers to the devastation and discover increased knowledge through Daniel's preserved book.

**two others** (v. 5)—two angels

**a time, times, and half a time** (v. 7)—an answer to the question of verse 6; adding these (one, two, and one-half) come to the final three and a half years of Daniel's 70th week (9:27), the time of trouble when the "little horn" or willful king persecutes the

<sup>13</sup> *"But you, go your way till the end; for you shall rest, and will arise to your inheritance at the end of the days."*

saints (7:25; see also 11:36–39 and Revelation 12:14; the same span is described by other phrases in Revelation 11:2, 3;13:5)

**Many . . . purified** (v. 10)— Salvation will come to many Jews during the Great Tribulation. The truly saved develop in godliness through trials; the unsaved pursue false values.

**the daily sacrifice** (v. 11)—a reference to the end of daily temple sacrifice, previously allowed under a covenant which the Antichrist formed with Israel, that he later causes to cease in the middle of the final seven years (9:27); then favorable relations give way to persecution; even his abomination that desecrates the temple is accompanied with persecution

**one thousand two hundred and ninety days** (v. 11)—From the intrusion of the abomination, there follow 1,290 days, including 1,260 which make up the last three and a half years of the final seven years. The extra thirty days allow for the judgment of the living subsequent to Christ's return before the Millennium and all its blessings begin.

**Blessed** (v. 12)—This is in the kingdom that gives blessedness after the subjugation to Gentile empires in chapters 2, 7, and 8.

**one thousand three hundred and thirty-five days** (v. 12)— Forty-five more days, even beyond the 1,290 days, allows for transition between Israel's time of being shattered (verse 7) and God's setting up of His kingdom (see 7:13, 14, 27).

**go** (v. 13)—Daniel's own career would soon involve death.

**will arise** (v. 13)—in resurrection

**at the end of the days** (v. 13)—The kingdom will ensue after prophesied days of 9:24–27 and 12:11–12.

# Understanding the Text

2) What does chapter 12 say the angel Michael will be doing during the awful period known as the Great Tribulation?

_____

_____

_____

_____

_____

3) What does verse 2 say about the doctrine of resurrection? What will happen to those who are made to "awake"? Verse 3 gives a glimpse of what eternity holds for believers? What is that?

_____

_____

_____

_____

_____

4) How did the "man clothed in linen" respond to Daniel's concern (verses 8–13)?

_____

_____

_____

_____

_____

_____

# Cross Reference

Read this passage from Revelation 20–21.

11 *Then I saw a great white throne and Him who sat on it, from whose face the earth and the heaven fled away. And there was found no place for them.*
12 *And I saw the dead, small and great, standing before God, and books were opened. And another book was opened, which is the Book of Life. And the dead were judged according to their works, by the things which were written in the books.*
13 *The sea gave up the dead who were in it, and Death and Hades delivered up the dead who were in them. And they were judged, each one according to his works.*
14 *Then Death and Hades were cast into the lake of fire. This is the second death.*
15 *And anyone not found written in the Book of Life was cast into the lake of fire.*

1 *Now I saw a new heaven and a new earth, for the first heaven and the first earth had passed away. Also there was no more sea.*
2 *Then I, John, saw the holy city, New Jerusalem, coming down out of heaven from God, prepared as a bride adorned for her husband.*
3 *And I heard a loud voice from heaven saying, "Behold, the tabernacle of God is with men, and He will dwell with them, and they shall be His people. God Himself will be with them and be their God.*
4 *"And God will wipe away every tear from their eyes; there shall be no more death, nor sorrow, nor crying. There shall be no more pain, for the former things have passed away."*
5 *Then He who sat on the throne said, "Behold, I make all things new." And He said to me, "Write, for these words are true and faithful."*
6 *And He said to me, "It is done! I am the Alpha and the Omega, the Beginning and the End. I will give of the fountain of the water of life freely to him who thirsts.*
7 *"He who overcomes shall inherit all things, and I will be his God and he shall be My son.*
8 *"But the cowardly, unbelieving, abominable, murderers, sexually immoral, sorcerers, idolaters, and all liars shall have their part in the lake which burns with fire and brimstone, which is the second death."*

# Exploring the Meaning

5)What does this passage in Revelation say about the final state of the righteous and the wicked? How does it amplify and expand the revelation given to Daniel?

_____

_____

_____

_____

_____

6) Read 1 Corinthians 3:8, 2 Thessalonians 1:12, and 1 Peter 5:10. What do these verses say about the idea of eternal rewards and believers being given the privilege of reflecting God's glory?

_____

_____

_____

_____

_____

# Summing Up . . .

"Hell will not be a place, as some jokingly envision, where the ungodly will continue to do their thing while the godly do theirs in heaven. Hell will have no friendships, no fellowship, no camaraderie, no comfort. It will not even have the debauched pleasures in which the ungodly love to revel on earth. There will be no pleasure in hell of any kind or degree—only torment, 'day and night forever and ever' (Revelation 20:10)." —*John MacArthur*

# Reflecting on the Text

7) Given the stark reality and certainty of coming judgment, how will you pray differently this week? For unsaved friends, neighbors, co-workers? For world leaders? Why doesn't this truth sober us more?

_____

_____

_____

_____

_____

_____

8) What changes should you make in how you live in light of the Scripture's teaching about eternal rewards for faithful earthly service?

_____

_____

_____

_____

_____

9) What two or three steps do you intend to take in the next month to better understand end-times prophecy?

_____

_____

_____

_____

# Recording Your Thoughts

_____

_____

_____

_____

_____

_____

_____

_____

_____

_____

_____

_____

_____

_____

_____

_____

_____

_____

_____

_____

## For further study, see the following passages:

| | | |
|---|---|---|
| Isaiah 26:20–21 | Jeremiah 30:7 | Zechariah 13:8–9 |
| Malachi 3:16—4:3 | Matthew 24:1, 21, 29–31 | Matthew 25:31–46 |
| Mark 13:14 | Luke 10:20 | John 5:28–29 |
| Romans 11:26 | 2 Thessalonians 2:3–4 | Jude 9 |
| Revelation 11:13 | Revelation 12:12–17 | Revelation 13:7–8 |
| Revelation 17:8 | | |

# *Additional Notes*